Freedom and the Moral Life

FREEDOM AND THE MORAL LIFE

The Ethics of
William James

by John K. Roth

THE WESTMINSTER PRESS
Philadelphia

STANDARD BOOK No. 664–20859–2
LIBRARY OF CONGRESS CATALOG CARD No. 69–17069

PUBLISHED BY THE WESTMINSTER PRESS ®
PHILADELPHIA, PENNSYLVANIA

PRINTED IN THE UNITED STATES OF AMERICA

for
Lynn and Andy

Preface

WILLIAM JAMES is a philosopher who is intrigued by the nature of change and permanence in human existence. This is reflected in his interest in man's freedom. James believes that our lives are permeated by a freedom that gives us the chance to shape the world that we inhabit. We can change our environment to suit many of our interests, and at the same time we can change ourselves through the choices that we make. On the other hand, the same freedom that allows us to initiate change raises a question that is striking in its permanence throughout human history. The question is this: If I am free to act in a variety of ways, how should I act and what values should I take to be the most important? Human freedom forces this moral question upon us, and although the circumstances in which it must be answered may vary from one generation to another, the question will always need to be faced.

This book focuses on the moral philosophy of William James, and it is written with the hope that it will stimulate reflection about some of the ethical issues raised by our freedom. James's philosophy provides a context for thought on these matters that is especially useful now. This is true because James both shares certain feelings of discontent with us and makes some suggestions that we can use to achieve a fresh and sound perspective about the moral life.

Man's awareness of freedom has led to a contemporary mood of suspicion about ethical absolutes, whether they rest in re-

ligious decrees or in rationalistic claims about a priori truths
and natural laws. Yet the present mood is also one of discontent, because it senses that rebellion against such absolutes is
not sufficient to solve the moral problems that we continue to
face. James shares these feelings with us. He rejects authorita-
rian and rationalistic absolutes, but he also sees that rebellion
is not enough and that we need to find sound principles to
guide our decisions in a moral direction. Moreover, his philosophy can provide a much-needed perspective that will aid us
in overcoming a current problem. After rejecting old ways of
thinking and asserting that new guidelines are needed, contemporary men are often unable to present a sound analysis
concerning what the new guidelines ought to be or what a
new view of the moral life ought to entail. James can help us to
find our way. His philosophy can aid us in finding sound guidelines and in seeing the structure of the moral life in a world of
freedom. The analysis and elaboration of James's philosophy in
the following chapters move toward these goals.

   Books are written in solitude, but they are the results of
social relationships. Many institutions and people have worked
to make this book possible, and I owe special thanks to the
following. I am indebted to Claremont Men's College for providing a stimulating atmosphere in which to think and teach
and for giving me a summer study grant to allow the comple-
tion of the manuscript. My thanks also goes to Prof. John Wild,
of Yale University. I was introduced to the philosophy of William James in a graduate seminar taught by Professor Wild at
Yale in the fall of 1964. He later directed my doctoral disserta-
tion, which focused on the problems raised in this book. Professor Wild is a persuasive teacher, and my book shows his
influence. I am also grateful to Prof. Frederick Sontag, of Po-
mona College. My friendship with him dates back to my days
as an undergraduate student, and it is a continuing source of
encouragement and joy. Professor Sontag urges a person to set
high goals. Moreover, he fosters the courage that it takes to try
to achieve them. He read the manuscript carefully, and his

suggestions helped to improve it. Finally, I am deeply indebted to my parents, who first taught me what freedom means, and above all to my wife, whose untiring help and growing love make life rich and meaningful.

J. K. R.

Claremont, California

Contents

I

William James
and Contemporary Life

A. James's Ethical Insights

WILLIAM JAMES (1842–1910) is one of the most important figures in the development of American thought. In particular his efforts in psychology and in philosophy have left lasting marks on America.[1] One reason for James's influence is that his intellectual pursuits deal with the practical problems of clarifying and implementing basic human values such as freedom, and eliminating destructive conflicts in both individual and communal life. The presence of these themes in all James's writings reveals that he takes a primary interest in moral issues.

Although ethical views play an important part in James's pragmatism, philosophy of religion, and metaphysics, the attempts to come to grips with his ethical philosophy have not been numerous.[2] This is due in part to the fact that, while James was greatly interested in ethical questions, he never developed a fully systematic ethical theory. He was more interested in describing a general ethical stance toward existence than in developing a system of rules or virtues. Thus, his insights into the moral life are scattered throughout his writings, and they are not unified as well as they might be.

The purpose of this study is to explore and develop the ethical insights that James's philosophy contains. Because of the unsystematic nature of his ethical perspective, a good deal of analysis and interpretation is required to bring out the basic elements of this aspect of his thought. The account developed here will clarify the key ideas at the roots of his view of the moral life and attempt to give a more unified statement of these ideas than James himself provides. In doing this, we will not only obtain an understanding of the thought of a man from our philosophical past, but we will also find that James is still a contemporary figure. He deals with problems that are very much a part of the present scene.

B. CURRENT ISSUES

As the following chapters will show, James's ethical philosophy revolves around his assumption that the most important values for men are those of freedom, on the one hand, and personal and social unity, on the other. In one way or another James deals continually with the relationships that must exist between these values if human life is to be full and rich. His suggestions on this score are not always fully developed, and at times his comments are ambiguous. However, in grappling with these relationships he is attempting to treat problems that are at the foundations of many contemporary difficulties.

The history of the American people involves a continuing attempt to find a workable relationship between freedom and the unity or order that is needed for full life at both the personal and communal levels. One goal of this quest is to prevent choices from becoming chaotic and narrowly selfish. Another aim is to prevent structure and order from becoming too restrictive. Full development of individual and communal life requires a fruitful tension between freedom, structure, and order, but maintenance of a proper balance between these factors is extremely difficult to achieve. Our national life at present exemplifies this fact. Phenomena such as Black Power and the student protests on college and university campuses suggest that there is widespread dissatisfaction about the existing relationships between freedom and unity. The unrest revealed in these movements is only part of the picture, however, for there is also the problem of how individuals and society ought to move in the face of the mood of protest and criticism. William James does not provide complete and ready-made answers to problems of this sort, but his philosophy does bring factors to light that men will have to take account of now, if they are to find a course of action that will preserve what is best in a democratic society. In this way James is a figure of contemporary importance.

There is another sense in which James is still important. His philosophy, especially with its stress on freedom, is striking in its similarities to two types of philosophical and religious thought that presently exert influence in this country. The first of these is existential philosophy and the second is situation ethics.

Existentialism is regarded by some as a philosophical import coming into America from European sources. Such a view, however, neglects the fact that many of the themes stressed in the existential literature are present in our own tradition. James's philosophy is a rich source of these motifs. In fact, the interest in existentialism in this country has led to a renewal of interest in James precisely because of the similarities that are found between the views of James and the existential thinkers.

The existential philosophies of men such as Søren Kierke-gaard, Martin Heidegger, Jean-Paul Sartre, and Maurice Merleau-Ponty are phenomenological in character. That is, they attempt to give a broad empirical description and analysis of the universal structures and characteristics of human existence as these are felt and lived through in experience. Not only does James share this descriptive and analytic concern with these men, but there is also considerable agreement in the particular accounts of human existence that are developed by the existential philosophers and by James.[3] These likenesses manifest themselves in at least four themes which can be noted briefly.

The first is that human consciousness is an intentional, selective force.[4] Two basic concepts are contained in this idea. First, we can point out that speaking of human consciousness as intentional means that this consciousness is a form of existence which is aware of being. To put the point in another way, so long as there is human consciousness there is awareness of something. Within the human sphere, this awareness can come to include a sophisticated self-consciousness, although in its primordial form our consciousness is for the most part turned outward toward the world rather than in on itself. In any case, consciousness is always an engaged awareness. It always has some content.

Secondly, an intentional relationship between consciousness and being also involves the idea that consciousness is an active and selective force helping to organize and structure being into the world that we know. Thus, on this view, consciousness is not a passive container simply absorbing and reproducing what is given. As a selective power, consciousness helps to constitute its content. One important ramification of this is that both our world and our personal existence are not complete so long as we live, but instead they are factors in an open-ended process and development.

The selective character of consciousness is at the foundation of a second theme shared by James and the existential philosophers. The idea of a selective consciousness suggests a strong sense of human freedom. Through the choices they make, men organize and structure their existence in many and varied ways. The world that we inhabit is sufficiently flexible to allow for a plurality of life-styles and forms of meaning. All of this leads naturally to the conclusion that we live in a world of freedom where meanings and values, as well as actions, can be shaped by free human decisions.

This view, of course, raises some basic questions about the nature and source of the moral standards or norms which individuals and communities have or seek. The tendency of James and the existential philosophers is to say that any ethical standards that exist are created out of experience rather than that they are fixed and given to a consciousness that is essentially passive. This stress on man's creative role in determining meanings and values, including those of an ethical sort, is related to a dissatisfaction with ethical absolutes or ideals that are imposed on human life from the outside. Both James and existential philosophers react against such absolutes, and this is revealed in their criticisms of natural-law theories and ethical appeals based solely on religious revelation.

However, if such absolutes are destroyed the question remains: What normative guidelines will there be? Unless a good deal of care is taken in solving this problem, the emphasis on freedom and creativity can lead to a radical subjectivism and a destructive relativism. In our own time, increasing violence, disrespect for law, and a general attitude that it is all right for everyone to "do his own thing" so long as no one else is directly injured are all indications that we have moved too far in the direction of the subjective and the relative. When these tendencies appear, they weaken the communal structure and the cooperation that is needed for a full and harmonious existence. An emphasis on the relations of free choices, values, and norms is important, but precautions must be taken to avoid dangerous excesses.

Put in broad terms, the accent on freedom that we have been noting raises this crucial question: Can we obtain a perspective that takes account of the role of choice in the determination of values and norms and that will at the same time guide our choosing so as to avoid a subjectivism that undercuts basic values in communal life? Working in the context of James's philosophy, we find it possible to develop a point of view that can help us to obtain such a perspective. James enables us to see what it means to be free in a world where a moral structure is not completely determined prior to our choosing, but where there are also basic boundaries which we ignore at our own risk.

A third existential theme that also plays a major role in James's thought deals with man's experience of his own finitude. Our existence in the world is highly flexible, but it is not infinitely so. The existence that we live and encounter contains a factor of resistance. In our encounter with this resistance we become aware of the fact that human life itself is limited and finite. We do not seem to have the power to fulfill all our desires, and we also lack an understanding of the boundaries of possibility and resistance. The quality of this finitude is captured in an idea shared by James and the existential philosophers, namely, that man is "thrown" into existence in such a way that he cannot get beyond it or outside it either in order to alter it in every respect or in order to understand it to his complete satisfaction.

The fact of man's "thrownness" has some important ramifications for the relationships between meaning and freedom. If a man is thrown into a world that is vast in possibilities and yet resistant, and if his presence in this world is finite and limited with respect to power and understanding, then every individual must face problems concerning the meaning of his own life. The boundaries of meaning may be established, but meaning itself will not be fixed for the individual. Since it is impossible to observe existence from the outside, choice and action from within will be required in order for existence to make sense. Meaning will be in a process of development from within existence as one lives, and meaning will ultimately be shaped and appropriated by individuals. To put this in another way, each man confronts this question: What does it mean to exist? Although men live communally, such a question calls for an answer from the individual. Communal styles of life may be of help here, but ultimately no one is in a position to answer for the individual, since every man's life begins with the ambiguous "thrownness" of birth and ends with a death beyond which no man sees with absolute clarity and finality.

The man who faces this human predicament honestly sees that human life involves a blending of risk and fallibility, which together constitute the final shared theme that we need to note. For human life to be meaningful, choices must be made, projects undertaken, and lives committed in a world that seems at least partly ambiguous. This world is one in which human understanding, knowledge, and reason are all touched by finitude. In such a world certainty is a rare commodity. Thus, appeals to self-evidence, finality, and absolute

truth must be replaced with appeals to experience that are
both empirical and fallible. Further, since human decisions
and actions are fallible, they are always attended by risk.
Error, failure, frustration, despair, and even death are some of
the risks that we face in trying to achieve meaning and success
in life. Human existence has a precarious, fragile quality with
which men must live. Attempts to escape this precariousness
will always fail in the end, and the highest human life will be
that of a man who cheerfully accepts risk in attempting to find
a meaningful pattern of existence for himself and the human
community.

The notions of human finitude, fallibility, and risk provide a
link between James and another facet of current thought,
namely, situation ethics. A situational approach to ethics is by
no means new. It has obvious relations to existential thought,
and it has been present in the American tradition for many
years through the pragmatism of men like James and John
Dewey.[5] However, the idea is discussed more now than in the
past, partly because of its growing influence in contemporary
theological and religious circles.[6]

Moving from the idea that certainty is scarce, particularly
with respect to claims about what is always right or wrong
ethically speaking, the thrust of situation ethics is to argue
that ethics does not consist primarily of rules that are made up
in advance and that are to be obeyed at all times. Rather,
ethics should focus both on general principles and on processes
of thought and action guided by those principles which will
produce fresh and fitting ethical solutions that are tailor-made
for particular situations. Men must act in terms of the highest
principles they can find, but applying these principles so as to
produce decisions that are ethically sound will require close
attention to the details of the circumstances under consideration and not slavish adherence to rules or policies totally determined in advance.

The negative view toward a rule orientation that characterizes situation ethics has been interpreted by some critics to be
both a general repudiation of communal ethical norms and
a movement toward a harmful subjectivism and relativism. On

the whole, however, this is a misunderstanding of the situational emphasis that capitalizes on the fact that there is a major difference between a principle and a rule. On the one hand, a rule (e.g., "Never tell lies") tells a person specifically what to do or what not to do. On the other hand, an ethical principle (e.g., "Love your neighbor as yourself") does not give such specific directives about conduct but, rather, suggests factors that ought to be taken into account in making a decision that will be ethically sound in the context of a particular situation. Rules may function in a principle-oriented ethics in the sense that they provide handy statements about what the community has generally found to be a beneficial course of action. In this understanding, rules function as communal generalizations which ought not to be broken or changed without good reasons. However, there may be times and places in which some of these rules will need to be broken. This points out that in a principle-oriented ethics, the principles standing behind the rules are the motivating factors for any rules that do exist, and the principles are of greater importance than the rules.

James is a proponent of an ethical view that is principle-oriented and situational in its approach to decision-making. He clarifies the nature of a situational approach to ethics, and he also helps to meet the criticism that such an orientation will have an undesirable subjectivism and relativism as its outcome. These ideas, plus others that we have noted thus far, will be developed more fully in the following chapters, but perhaps enough has been said already to indicate that a study of the ethical philosophy of William James is a timely undertaking. In analyzing James's ideas and in criticizing and expanding them where necessary, we may obtain some guidance for our own problems and situations.

C. The Method of Consideration

We will be exploring James's writings in the next five chapters in order to bring his ethical position to light. As already suggested, there is a basic problem in dealing with

James's ethics due to the fact that his treatment of ethical problems is widely scattered in his writings, which cover a period of some forty years. In analyzing James's philosophy we will generally deal with his works in the order in which they were written and published. There are two main reasons for using this approach. The first is that this method of dealing with his literature will most easily allow us to trace the important connections that James sees between human freedom and the selective powers of consciousness. An understanding of James's ethics requires clarity about this relationship. The relationship is established in his early writings, including *The Principles of Psychology,* which appeared in 1890, and thus it makes sense to begin by considering these works.

A second reason for a chronological ordering is related to the fact that there is a movement in James's thought from an emphasis on the individual and his choices and demands to a greater consideration of the whole human community and the effect of individual choices on it. In particular, James's idea of freedom develops in relation to social and religious ideals that are filled in only when we reach a work such as *The Varieties of Religious Experience,* which appeared in 1902. However, these later developments are clearly understood only against the background of the early essays and *The Principles of Psychology.*

II

Consciousness and Selfhood in *The Principles of Psychology* and Early Essays, 1875–1890

A. JAMES'S PSYCHOLOGY

OUR TASK in this chapter will be to explore James's understanding of the nature of consciousness and selfhood. The emphasis will be on the selective character of consciousness, and this account will help to provide the necessary foundation for clarification of the ideals of freedom and unity that are at the heart of James's moral philosophy.

We will begin with a few introductory remarks about James's writings from 1875 to 1890. In this period James's efforts were devoted to a two-volume work called *The Principles of Psychology* and to a variety of papers and essays on philosophical and psychological topics. These papers include "Reflex Action and Theism," "The Dilemma of Determinism," "The Sentiment of Rationality," and "Great Men and Their Environment." They are important in our discussion because they focus on questions dealing with the selective capacity of consciousness, the nature of human freedom and reason, and the task of finding meaning in existence.

James worked for about twelve years on *The Principles of Psychology,* and it still stands as a landmark in its field. One of the interesting features of the book is that, like the essays noted, it deals with many fundamental philosophical problems. Issues concerning the nature of consciousness and reason, the debate between freedom and determinism, the relation of the mind and the body, and "necessary truths" are in its chapters. As James pushes psychology toward the goal of making it a natural science, he never fails to recognize that psychology and philosophy stand close together with respect to the problems that they treat.

There is another sense in which psychology and philosophy are closely related in James's mind. He believes that these disciplines should share a broadly empirical approach in attempting to solve the problems that they face. Attempts to solve problems through a priori speculation frequently lead to forms of dogmatism and reduction that distort the experience and the facts under consideration. Philosophers have often been guilty of these tendencies, but James also points out that there can be dogmatism and reduction when a natural science claims to be empirical but is actually too narrow in its outlook. James's version of empiricism, which he sometimes calls *radical empiricism,* urges us to start with the experiences of men as they are actually felt and lived through, rather than immediately fitting these experiences into theories and frameworks that we have developed in advance. Theories and conceptual frameworks are valuable tools, but they must not be used at the expense of an open and sensitive investigation of the experiences themselves.

The psychologist ought to be a sympathetic observer who tries to see and understand the experiences of men as they are felt by individuals. Moreover, the science of psychology ought to include disciplined descriptions of the life of consciousness just as much as theoretical explanations. In fact, description is crucial to explanation and the discovery of possible causal regularities. Before we can explain experience or find genuine causal connections in it, we must have accurate descriptions of the experiences in question. Thus, early in *The Principles of Psychology* James characterizes the science of psychology in the following way: "Psychology is the Science of Mental Life, both of its phenomena and their conditions. The phenomena are such things as we call feelings, desires, cognitions, reasonings, decisions, and the like."[7] James is interested in the phenomena as well as in the conditions for them. Much of his time is devoted to the descriptive task of clarifying these phenomena, and his findings will be important for us.

James's belief in the significance of sympathetic observation and description of the life of consciousness is coupled with his view that an introspective method is of primary importance.[8] James is aware of the problems that introspection raises in the attempt both to understand others and to draw universal conclusions about human existence. Thus, he argues for the fallibility of the findings obtained through introspection, and on occasion he refuses to conclude anything from his studies except that something seems to be the case for him personally. Still, he urges the usefulness of introspection, provided that precautions are taken to prevent distortions and overly subjective interpretations of the data under investigation.

James warns against what he takes to be one of the most devastating errors that may plague a descriptive psychology in general and an introspective orientation in particular. He calls this error the "psychologist's fallacy."[9] This error occurs most frequently when the investigator attributes a particular content and awareness to the conscious state under consideration when that content and awareness is really present only in the experience of the investigator qua investigator. As James says: "We must be very careful therefore, in discussing a state of mind from the psychologist's point of view, to avoid foisting into its own ken matters that are only there for ours. We must avoid substituting what we know the consciousness *is*, for what it is a consciousness *of*, and counting its outward, and so to speak physical, relations with other facts of the world, in among the objects of which we set it down as aware."[10] Only by constantly guarding against these tendencies through self-criticism and reexamination can the investigator be sure that his findings will approximate the actual experience being described.

B. The Nature of Consciousness

One feature of James's view of human consciousness is of special importance, especially in regard to his understanding of freedom. This is the fact that James understands consciousness to be a choosing and a selecting agency which is stretched out in time.[11] Consciousness is always engaged in and interested in the world. It helps to structure and organize the world by attending to some factors, being partial to them, and at the same time ignoring others. Whether consciousness is at the highest stages of self-awareness or at the lowest prelinguistic, prereflexive levels of feeling, this selective process is going on.

In making these suggestions about consciousness, James is attacking all theories of human experience that regard the subject primarily as a passive knower or detached spectator. Consciousness is always active in his view, and in its higher forms its primary purpose is to formulate and to pursue goals and projects that have the effect of changing the environment that consciousness inhabits. Consciousness is a source of novelty. The interests that arise with various forms of life are unique contributions to the total world, and apart from the conscious beings involved, these interests qua interests would not exist at all.[12]

At times James describes the selective function of consciousness in such a way that he seems to be a radical subjectivist and voluntarist. For example, he says at one point, "Out of what is in itself an undistinguishable, swarming *continuum*, devoid of distinction or emphasis, our senses make for us, by attending to this motion and ignoring that, a world full of contrasts, or sharp accents, or abrupt changes, of picturesque light and shade."[13] And a little later in the same context a similar idea appears: "The mind chooses to suit itself, and decides what particular sensation shall be held more real and valid than all the rest."[14] Such statements imply that there is no order in the environment apart from that imposed by consciousness itself. However, it is not James's intention to make his suggestions so strong. He frequently argues for the independent reality of relations and conjunctions that are ordered and regular.

These relations between things are empirically experienced, and they constitute a part of the factor of resistance that we noted in Chapter I. Although there is still the need for selection to occur to produce all the details of the world that we know, the selective powers of consciousness are not omnipotent. Thus, seemingly radical passages like those above ought to be read as merely emphasizing James's belief that consciousness is operative in helping to create the particular world that we know and experience. It need not be the case that this participation is always consciously willed or that consciousness selects from a total chaos. It is sufficient to say that the order of the environment has a flexibility and a richness that permit a plurality of possibilities and genuine novelty in regard to its experienced character. James wants to account for the different worlds delineated by various forms of consciousness, and, while this implies a flexibility in being itself, total disorder is not necessitated.

James's stress on the selective powers of consciousness has some important ethical ramifications. We live in a world that ultimately forces us to choose, and we are therefore largely responsible for the quality and meaning of our existence in both its personal and communal dimensions. However, it is often difficult for us to choose well, and two factors play a major part in this fact. First, since human consciousness is a selective force, it can and does show a tendency to be partial and exclusive. In selecting or attending to something, we are forced to ignore some other features of the world.[15] Thus, we may find not only that there are times when the positive content of consciousness leads to detrimental effects but that the factors we ignore may be the most crucial to our well-being. A second point related to the first is that it is generally the case that the selective consciousness of the individual is not isolated but, rather, is engaged in a community. Since there is no prearranged harmony among the selections we make, our choices may place limitations on ourselves and others, and this can create conflicts and problems of huge proportions.

Fortunately, men can do some things to regulate the narrowing tendencies in human consciousness that destroy harmonious relationships. In fact, ethical reflection consists largely in trying to broaden our conscious awareness so that we can avoid fragmentation and chaos. The selective and often partial character of consciousness does not preclude the possibility that one's attention can be directed to concerns of a broad moral nature. Consciousness can and does have a moral character because we are able to decide what to attend to and what to ignore. Further, our decisions about these issues can be guided by the ideal of an environment that maximizes the possibilities for a creative use of our powers and that at the same time minimizes the tendencies toward destructive conflicts.

C. The Efficacy of Consciousness

James's emphasis on the selectivity of consciousness and the vast difference this power seems to make in our experience forced him to come to terms with the proponents of another view of consciousness with which he disagreed. Some of James's contemporaries made strong and exclusive claims for a theory of consciousness known as *epiphenomenalism*. Epiphenomenalism is the view that consciousness is merely a by-product of physiological processes. Although consciousness accompanies these processes, it is in no way active as a causal factor in the determination of future conduct. Consciousness makes no real difference to the events that are taking place. According to this view, a human life is essentially a series of determined physiological activities, and, in spite of all appearances to the contrary, phenomena such as choices and feelings are only the impotent resultants of these activities. James calls this theory of consciousness the "automaton theory." He feels that the advocates of the theory make dogmatic claims, and therefore he devotes a chapter of *The Principles of Psychology* to an attack on the theory and to a presentation of some arguments defending the view that consciousness is efficacious. It is important for us to note what James has to say about these matters, for his views play a part in his understanding of man's freedom. Unless a defense can be found for the idea that consciousness is efficacious, it will be meaningless to talk about human freedom.

James attacks epiphenomenalism by arguing that we do not need to take the theory as finally binding, because it rests on assumptions that are subject to basic criticisms.[16] First, he points out that the claim that epiphenomenalism is the only respectable theory about consciousness is defended by an argument based on an inconclusive appeal to continuity. On the grounds that some animal behavior can be understood adequately without positing consciousness as an active force, it is assumed that all animal behavior, including that of men, can be understood without an appeal to the causal efficacy of consciousness. But, James points out, this way of thinking is inconclusive because it moves too quickly from the particular to the universal. In fact, if we allow such rapid leaps, we can make this line of thought work in the opposite direction as well. For example, we might argue that in order to understand some human action we do have to regard consciousness as efficacious in determining what happens. Moving on from that position, we might maintain that an adequate understanding of any animal behavior always requires an appeal to causal efficacy of consciousness. These arguments from continuity can battle with each other indefinitely without being finally conclusive. Thus, insofar as the epiphenomenalist's position is based on such an appeal to continuity, it ought not to be regarded as finally binding but rather as one possible hypothesis to be further tested in experience.

Secondly, James thinks that the epiphenomenalist's position is inconclusive because it rests on a tenuous belief fostered by the aesthetic appeal of simplicity. Because it is thought to be simpler or more convenient for a disciplined scientific investigation to deal with purely physical matters, rather than having to contend with something so elusive as consciousness, it is believed that this warrants the dismissal of references to consciousness in the causal explanation of behavior. James questions the legitimacy of assuming that everything in nature is fixed for the convenience of an investigation that is oriented in this way, especially when the experience that men live through from day to day seems to reveal the activity of consciousness so strongly.

Finally, in a third point related to the second, James notes that the attractiveness of epiphenomenalism has been due in part to the difficulty of conceptualizing how consciousness might exert causal influence. But, James argues, ever since David Hume presented his analysis of causality there has been a good deal of vagueness about all sorts of relationships that we regard as causal. Thus, it is a mistake to assume that we have a clear and rigorous concept of causality that applies only in the physical realm. Our present concept of causation is a general notion referring either to the constant conjunction of events or to the production of effects. Both of these conceptions are sufficiently broad to allow us to speak of causal relations involving consciousness. Until such time as a rigorous clarification of the concept of causation forces us to rule out the possibility of speaking of consciousness as causally efficacious, we ought to continue to operate with the idea that consciousness is a causal force, for this is clearly the view that a commonsense understanding of experience imposes upon us.

Having argued that epiphenomenalism is at best a weakly supported hypothesis, James turns to some data from evolution that provide strong evidence in favor of the efficacy of consciousness. The most important point that he makes in this context stems from some of his observations about different forms of life. James notes that the animals that have the most highly developed forms of consciousness seem to have nervous systems that are correspondingly flexible. In these organisms there is a relative lack of certainty about how they will respond in situations. The relationship is reversed in organisms with less highly developed forms of consciousness. Their nervous systems are less flexible and generally unable to make the wide variety of responses characteristic of the organisms with less stable nervous systems and more highly developed forms of consciousness. Hence there is greater certainty about their responses in particular circumstances. James does not think that these relationships are merely coincidental. In order to obtain specific guidance for survival and development, the organisms with highly flexible nervous systems would seem to require something additional to help determine action. If consciousness were efficacious, it would provide the needed function of selection and goal direction. Since there are many organisms which do have life-styles that combine flexible nervous systems with consistent goal-directed conduct, James believes that there is considerable evidence in support of the view that consciousness is causally efficacious.

In particular, James finds his study of human consciousness and the human nervous system pointing in this direction. His study and knowledge of brain processes lead him to conclude that the human brain is extremely flexible. While there is structure in the brain, James thinks that "the brain is an instrument of possibilities, but of no certainties."[17] Thus, the brain requires exactly what selective consciousness seems to offer, namely, determination of action through attention and choice. This activity of consciousness seems to be illustrated in common experience. For example, in problem situations, where habit or automatic nerve-processes are the most hesitant, conscious awareness and exertion of thought usually are the most intense. James grants that this evidence is circumstantial, but he believes that it points clearly in the direction of the view that consciousness does make a causal difference in our experience.

James sees that if human consciousness is regarded as an epiphenomenon strictly caused by physiological processes and exerting no causal influence, then the usefulness of feeling and knowledge becomes questionable, since they do not exist apart from consciousness. But if empirical observation points anywhere, it points toward the fact that these factors are extremely useful to us, precisely because they enable us to guide our activity in the future and help us to make choices that are sound. This is even implied in the interest of the proponents of epiphenomenalism in gaining acceptance for their theory. Presumably, knowledge about and adoption of their position make some practical difference in our lives. Otherwise, all of the debate and argumentation is robbed of significance. However, the very meaning of asserting and arguing about the epiphenomenal view seems to undercut the theory, for in order for our understanding to make a practical difference, consciousness must be efficacious.

James does not claim to have given exhaustive proof of the fact that consciousness is causally efficacious. His analysis is directed both toward preventing dogmatic answers to the question and toward presenting evidence in favor of the hypothesis that he feels best suits our understanding and our needs. His view that consciousness is efficacious supports the possibility of morality by urging that choices and decisions are determining factors in human conduct. Moreover, a broad moral choice is involved in deciding for or against the view that consciousness is efficacious. The possible answers that can be given on this issue contain important implications about the value and meaning of existence. James thinks it is important to pick a solution that provides the greatest meaning and order for our lives, and in this case he has little doubt that belief in the efficacy of consciousness is proper.

D. SELFHOOD

Consciousness makes a difference to human life through its selective powers. These powers lead men to focus their attention and energy on a wide variety of things. In many instances our selections are alike, but there is one crucial respect in which each man organizes the world differently, namely, in his division of the world into what is *myself* and what is *not-myself.* Thus, a study of human consciousness leads naturally to a study of the self. James's treatment of selfhood has two facets that are significant for our purposes. The first involves his attempt to handle questions concerning personal identity, and the second involves his attempt to describe the content of our concept of self.

Personal Identity

Experience is always owned. It belongs to someone, but the nature of this ownership is not easy to determine. One of the reasons for this is that a human life is at the same time continuous and changing. James strives to understand this puzzling fact without resorting to Hume's view that the self consists of atomistic sense impressions and ideas bound together by forces of association. He also rejects the rationalistic conceptions of a transcendental ego or a soul postulated to account for personal identity. James cannot accept Hume's account because he finds that the attempt to build experience and the self out of primal atomistic sense impressions is an artificial construction that has no basis in lived experience. Hume's empiricism falls short because it fails to take account of the immediate relational features of all experience. With Hume in mind James says: "Most books start with sensations, as the simplest mental facts, and proceed synthetically, constructing each higher stage from those below it. But this is abandoning the empirical method of investigation. No one ever had a simple sensation by itself. Consciousness, from our natal day, is of a teeming multiplicity of objects and relations, and what we call simple sensations are results of discriminative attention, pushed often to a very high degree."[18] At the same time, James rejects the conceptions of the soul and the transcendental ego because they are arrived at by a needless speculation that posits entities that are not empirically grounded.

James believes that by close observation of experience we can find a more adequate way in which to understand the change and continuity that we experience. His suggestion is that we ought to view consciousness on the model of a stream that carries the past along with it as it flows into the future. The flowing of this stream is actually felt by us with respect to both its continuity and its change. The stream of consciousness is always moving and changing, but at the same time its contents are always relationally structured and continuous. To use James's term, consciousness has the power to "appropriate" past experiences and to focus its attention on the past as well as in the present and toward the future. Consciousness flows in such a way that, in addition to feeling its own present existence, each pulse of consciousness is cognitive of something that has gone before. As James says, "Each Thought is thus born an owner, and dies owned, transmitting whatever it realized as its Self to its own later proprietor."[19]

If the stream of consciousness involves a gradual shifting of experience and attention in which some common ingredients are always retained, one of the most important of these ingredients is bodily feeling. Some bodily feeling is always involved in our conscious life, and our conscious awareness is always shaped by the fact that it is an embodied consciousness.[20] James is no advocate of a radical mind-body dualism. We cannot regard the body as a simple object from which we can divorce ourselves. Although the body may not always be at the center of attention, it is always on the fringes of experience. We can never totally escape our bodies in our present existence, and the conscious body as a unity is at the core of our personal identity.

There is an important ethical implication in James's idea of a stream of consciousness. It involves the fact that in its fullest sense the identity or unity of a human life is not something that is guaranteed from start to finish. Human life is an ongoing process. The achievement of a full and meaningful sense of identity is a task covering a lifetime. The reason for this is that the power of appropriation in the stream of consciousness involves a man's capacities for self-conscious organization of experience. Experience always leaves its mark on us, but the precise quality of that mark is partly determined by our free reactions to and organizations of experience. A harmonious, unified life requires taking over experience in such a way that there is an honest facing of it and a projection of future goals that does not try to deny its existence. This unity is not easy to achieve. For example, the past often haunts us in ways that threaten us and call our future plans and goals into question. Thus, I may try to escape my past by denying or repressing it, but if I do this, I make a choice that may seriously threaten my own identity. There is a factor of resistance in the self just as there is in other dimensions of the world that we inhabit. My past may be compatible with many possible movements into the future, but not with all, and if I choose dishonestly I may lose myself.

James's "Field Theory" of Selfhood

The second facet of James's interest in selfhood consists of his attempts to clarify the content of our empirical concept of *self*. What emerges is a "field theory" of selfhood. The self extends outward from a center in the powers of the conscious body into a world of objects and social relations. The result is that selfhood is a concept whose meaning can vary with the focus of attention. In illustrating this idea, James speaks of three aspects of selfhood which he calls the material self, the social self, and the spiritual self.

James's idea of the material self suggests that it is not always easy to draw a hard-and-fast boundary between what is *myself* and what is simply *mine*. We are related to our material possessions, our families, our homes, and even our bodies in such a way that we can use the words "my" or "mine" in conjunction with them. In many of the cases where we use these terms, we can conceive of the self as being separated from them, and yet our identification with these components of our lives is often so close that we do not distinguish ourselves from them completely. This is illustrated in situations where we experience the loss of these components. We actually feel that we have lost part of ourselves when we lose some part of them. In these cases James says there is "a sense of the shrinkage of our personality, a partial conversion of ourselves to nothingness, which is a psychological phenomenon by itself."[21] Consciousness is not an isolated entity, but rather is related to the world in such a way that the boundaries between the self and the world are not absolutely clear in every instance. This quality of consciousness can lead persons to adopt different styles of life and patterns of understanding which will need to achieve some accommodation with each other if destructive conflict is to be avoided.

These themes are developed further in conjunction with the social self, which is a second factor in James's "field theory." The understanding of who and what we are is not isolated from the influence of and interaction with other people. My encounter with you and your encounter with me will change both of us. As long as we deal with each other there will be this mutual interaction. Thus, even though there is a plurality of personal streams of consciousness, the exact boundaries between them are not absolutely clear at every point.

One of the influences of our interactions with others that interests James especially is that we come to see ourselves in terms of social functions that we perform or in terms of social roles that we play. The same person may see himself primarily as father, husband, employer, or employee, depending on the context he is in and on the other people who are at the focus of his attention. James believes that all of us have a variety of social selves, and if a life is to be free of frustration and conflict, there will need to be a harmonious relationship among them. Successful movement in this direction will also require coming to terms with the critical evaluations that other men make of us in the community. One will have to decide how to react to such evaluations, and James urges that the ideal goal to be achieved lies between two extreme reactions that men sometimes make. We can try to close ourselves off from the community and act as though it did not exist, or we can conform to the desires of others so much that we lose all individual integrity. What is needed instead is a middle path in which the individual seeks to find himself in the community without at the same time sacrificing the distance between it and himself that may be required for personal freedom and growth.

Efforts at personal growth and development will be facilitated if a man lives in a communal environment that values both the freedom of the individual to seek a meaningful pattern for his own life and at the same time cultivates an atmosphere that is free of destructive conflict. Freedom and social unity are needed for the development of the personal unity of purpose that makes existence meaningful. Failure to fulfill any of these conditions can result in a chaos that is destructive of meaning.

The pursuit of meaning and value in individual lives is related to the third aspect of selfhood that James notes. He calls this dimension the spiritual self. James does not intend the term "spiritual" to be construed in terms of a soul substance or a transcendental ego. Instead he uses the term more broadly in referring to "the *active* element in all consciousness."[22] This element is what we refer to when we speak of our abilities to think, make moral choices, and exert effort.[23] It is the source of attention and action. In short, although James does not make the connection explicit in this context, the spiritual self involves the capacities that constitute our freedom.

In the next chapter there will be more to say about James's understanding of freedom, but it requires a few comments now. Freedom is a concept that has many dimensions, and at this point James is hinting at one of its basic features. Freedom is rooted in our capacities for paying attention, thinking, choosing and exerting effort. As we become self-aware, we recognize that these capacities for purposeful activity are the very factors that make us human and free. We also come to recognize that freedom can grow or be lost and that it must be cultivated and protected. If we impair our conscious powers, our freedom is diminished. By the same token, careful cultivation of our capacities increases opportunity and freedom. Maximizing our capacities for thought, choice, and action maximizes our freedom. Of course, there is another dimension to this development of capacities, namely, creation of an environment that allows us to use these capacities in the pursuit of goals of our own choosing and with a genuine chance to fulfill the choices that we make. At this point freedom becomes a concept with more direct social and political features, and we will have more to say about these aspects later on.

James notes that, when men think critically and place a value on all three of the dimensions of selfhood we have been considering, the spiritual self stands highest.[24] In other words, the most valuable aspects of human life are our capacities to think, choose, and act, which really is to speak of our freedom. This freedom is at the core of selfhood. It is what makes us human persons. But even though we may single out these capacities for special importance in our understanding of selfhood, they are never isolated from the other dimensions we have noted. The capacities are themselves features of our conscious bodies, and they extend into a wide field of social relationships and activities in the world. These capacities of freedom would not exist in their present form without these other factors. Thus, in one way or another, selfhood involves all of these dimensions. It is a flexible empirical concept whose meaning varies as one extends or narrows the point of focus. In the most refined sense it refers to the capacities that constitute our freedom, but it can be broadened out to include much more.

E. Freedom, Unity, and Meaning

The study of James's view of consciousness and selfhood emphasizes the centrality and importance of selection and freedom. Such selection may be prereflexive or it may manifest itself in the self-conscious use of the powers to choose, think, and act which James takes to be at the core of selfhood. These powers are especially important from an ethical point of view, for it is through a creative use of the freedom they provide that ethical values and norms will be developed.

We have also noted James's suggestions that meaning functions at two basic levels, the personal and the social. His development of the idea of selfhood reveals the individual to be a field of concerns. The individual develops and cares for his projects and goals. If conflict and chaos are to be avoided in his life and choices, however, his finite projects need to be fitted into a broad horizon of purpose that can hold and order them. Personal unity of purpose is required. Without such unity inner conflict will result.

The chances are great that the pursuit of personal unity will be frustrated unless there is a high degree of social unity as well. If there is an environment that fosters mutual respect for persons and social harmony, an atmosphere of freedom in which meaning can be found is likely to prevail. The task of achieving such an environment raises important ethical questions concerning the limits on choice in a communal setting and how decisions ought to be made about this point. These issues will be dealt with in later chapters.

III

Freedom, Knowledge, and Value
in *The Principles of Psychology*
and Early Essays, 1875–1890

JAMES IS GREATLY interested in problems concerning the reality and nature of human freedom. The task of this chapter will be to develop his concept of freedom and to explain its importance for his understanding of the nature of knowledge and value. James's theory of consciousness suggests that consciousness is a free and selective force and that the existence of man and his world is shaped and influenced by its action. James interprets this to mean that knowledge and value emerge from a creative interaction between a man and his environment. His analysis of freedom leads to the view that knowledge and value are not passively received but actively sought out and created. In our development of these ideas it is important for us to begin by examining James's defense against theories of determinism that question the reality of human freedom.

A. James's Defense Against Determinism

Earlier we noted James's arguments for the efficacy of consciousness. However, it is one thing to argue that consciousness is efficacious and another to defend the view that the acts of consciousness are not parts of a rigidly determined sequence. James works to defend a theory of freedom against deterministic views, and his arguments rest primarily on the moral importance of a belief in freedom.

James casts the issue between the proponents of freedom and the determinists in terms of some of his psychological categories. His understanding of the issue between the two camps is this: "It relates solely to the amount of effort of attention or consent which we can at any time put forth."[25] The question is whether we have a free control over these factors in the present act of attending, or whether a given act of attending is caused in all its details by factors preceding and necessarily leading up to it. Scientifically speaking, James believes that the issue cannot be finally settled, because once a certain amount of attention is given, it is no longer possible to prove in any rigorous fashion whether or not more or less attention might have been given.[26] The exact situation cannot be duplicated for further observation and testing.

However, there may be other factors that are relevant to the positions we will take on the issue between freedom and determinism. Although James believes that a formal proof cannot be generated to settle the debate, placing the issue in a broader and more ethically oriented perspective may bring important factors to light. The moral features that James wants to point out are developed in some of the essays that he wrote in the period under consideration in this chapter. One good example is "The Dilemma of Determinism."[27]

Two closely related points stand out in this essay. First, James asks what it means to us if we are free. His answer is that freedom means that possibilities are real. Actions in the past do not necessarily determine actions in the present and the future. One of the things that James understands this to mean in human life is that our present conscious awareness is a factor of novelty which takes our experience in directions that are sometimes surprising. This awareness is influenced by factors in its past, but it is not exhaustively determined by them. It has an autonomy and a power of its own. This does not mean that the causal connections and regularities noted by the sciences are violated, but rather that these relationships may be taken over into a broader horizon of meaning constituted by free human choices. Causal regularity is needed to lead to determinate goals. If consciousness is a capacity for knowledge and novelty as James suggests, these causal relationships may become the means to the ends that we choose. Thus, the freedom that James is interested in does not result in an attack on appeals to causal regularities and laws, so long as we do not lapse into the confusion of thinking that these regularities and laws are totally exhaustive in their power to determine meanings, goals, and actions. James believes that if such determination does exist, the striving that constitutes full human life becomes a sham. Life is robbed of the significance that it is strongly felt to have.

These initial suggestions can be extended to say more about scientific investigations and their relation to the freedom-determinism debate. James sees that many of the proponents of determinism are influenced by the progress of scientific explorations, which rest on cause-and-effect analyses. They take these investigations to corroborate the view that any event in the world, including human behavior, is necessarily determined solely by factors in its past. James, however, believes that this conclusion is drawn too quickly, not only because the determination of human behavior cannot be experimentally proven, as noted above, but because the very meaning of the scientific enterprise itself rests on our being free. Even when he looks for the causal patterns that we have noted, the lived experience of the man engaged in scientific inquiry involves the feeling both that his project is only one possibility among many that might be pursued and that he has chosen his project freely out of a plurality of possibilities.

Not only does the significance of a man's scientific activities depend on freedom, but we can also say that the world that science uncovers emerges out of a broader horizon of experience. Scientific investigations are attempts to understand aspects of existence by focusing our attention in particular ways. These investigations abstract from a broader and richer, and perhaps more ambiguous, level of experience in which human activity is felt and interpreted as free. This broad horizon of experience is, in fact, a world of freedom. This world of freedom can be investigated from the particular perspective that is constituted by the interests and methods of the scientific inquiries. The findings of these investigations may be of tremendous importance and value in the pursuit of human goals, but the claims of the sciences and the philosophical implications, such as determinism, that may be extrapolated from them can become dogmatic and restrictive if we do not remember that these findings are themselves products of a chosen perspective.

James cautions us against assuming too easily that scientific inquiries, which may involve certain assumptions concerning uniform and determined causal sequences, provide us with a fully adequate picture of reality. The selectivity of consciousness, which focuses on certain parts of the world in terms of special interests, operates in the sciences. Assumptions concerning deterministic relationships and even the discovery of causal regularities do not exhaust our world, and a nonreductive understanding of human experience will require us to place scientific investigations in a broader perspective that leaves freedom standing.

The feeling that in the present moment we may choose freely from among a plurality of possibilities is related to a second point in James's essay. James thinks that the broad world of lived experience from which science abstracts contains a basic and widespread moral outlook that he calls *meliorism*. This is the view that the world may be morally improved if men do their part now and in the future. The world does not have to exhibit the moral imperfections that may presently exist. On the other hand, there is also the feeling that there is no absolute guarantee that the undesirable components will be removed and replaced with something better. Meliorism implies a world that is open-ended, where the past does not exhaustively determine what will be the case in the future, and where man's present conscious awareness has power and freedom to move in a variety of ways. If this power and freedom are properly used, human life can be made better. But there will be no progress without man's effort and his willingness to take risks.

This moral orientation is often at the roots of the particular choices that we make and the projects that we pursue, and the meaning and the significance of acts based on this moral orientation rest on the belief that the human world is a world of freedom. However, if determinism holds, the feeling of moral striving is frustrated. As James suggests, there are no real moral sides in a world of determinism, and yet our feeling is that the selective character of consciousness constantly pushes us in the direction of taking sides in a world where there are real options from among which we must choose. The only way to break the world up into the components of good and evil that we feel is to regard it as containing elements of freedom and possibility. Only in such a pluralistic world can the basic sense of moral striving be retained.

A deterministic universe creates a massive conflict with our moral understanding. For this reason James has no hesitation about branding determinism as a view that is irrational. This charge is based on his view of the nature of rationality.[28] James disagrees with the determinists who equate the domain of rationality with the domain of scientific methods, assumptions, and findings. He believes that when we talk about rationality we are speaking about something broader. In human life, which is always finite and fallible, the identifying mark of rationality is a human feeling of rest and peace that is the result of obtaining solutions to problems through an open consideration of experience. The components that figure in this "sentiment of rationality" are varied. Factors of logical consistency, systematic gathering and ordering of data, and critical analysis are involved. Appeals to our strongest ethical, aesthetic, and religious feelings may also be included. Thus, given two views that are logically sound and factually supported, the one that best fills ethical, aesthetic, and religious cravings in men will and ought to be regarded as the more rational. If we abstract from ethical, aesthetic, and religious considerations, James believes that freedom and determinism constitute two views about the world that are reasonable. However, if we recognize that rationality does include those considerations as well, the scales are tipped in favor of freedom. Freedom fits harmoniously with our sense of moral striving in a flexible universe, and determinism directly conflicts with this factor.

As was the case in his arguments for the efficacy of consciousness, James admits that, although these points are good reasons for belief in freedom, they do not constitute a conclusive proof of its reality. If determinism cannot be rigorously demonstrated, the same is also true for freedom. Thus, these views are best understood as postulates about the world's nature that are full of moral significance. James contends that when a person is faced by such postulates and conclusive proof is not forthcoming, he has the right and the responsibility to choose in favor of the view that best makes sense of his own existence. A man continues to live even when objective evidence is incomplete. In these cases the sensible thing to do is to consider the facts that are available and then choose the course of belief and action that best fits one's attempts to carve out a meaningful version of existence.

One of James's important philosophical contributions is to call attention to this relationship between a positive belief in the reality of freedom and the act of choosing. This relationship is even illustrated in an incident from James's life. When he was about thirty years old, he went through a difficult period in coming to a personal decision about the question of human freedom. His account of the outcome is significant. "I think that yesterday was a crisis in my life. I finished the first part of Renouvier's second *Essais* and see no reason why his definition of free will—'the sustaining of a thought *because I choose to* when I might have other thoughts'—need be the definition of an illusion. At any rate, I will assume for the present—until next year—that it is no illusion. My first act of free will shall be to believe in free will."[29]

Belief in freedom ultimately comes as the result of a definite choice on the part of the individual, and James thinks that this is peculiarly fitting.[30] In the light of the fact that conclusive evidence is not available for deciding the freedom-determinism issue on objective grounds, the possibility that either position might be true remains open. But if freedom is a reality, it is appropriate that a choice is required in regard to our belief in it. Freedom implies a freely chosen attitude toward itself. If we are free, there is no necessity about our belief in or recognition of freedom. If we ask, Are we free? the answer may be either yes or no. A conscious choice does not prove freedom's reality, but it is a factor that is required if a man is to view himself as free in the face of possible arguments to the contrary. By making such a choice, a man asserts himself in the direction of freedom.

James says: "Freedom's first deed should be to affirm itself. We ought never to hope for any other method of getting at the truth if indeterminism be a fact."[31] If we are to understand our existence as free, the logic of the situation requires us to choose rather than wait for the objective evidence of detached investigation to settle the issue with finality. But the choice is not based on an irrational, subjective desire. Instead, it rests on a reasoned analysis of a moral dilemma concerning life's meaning and on careful reflection about what the nature of freedom itself would require.

B. The Nature of Freedom

In Chapter II we noted that freedom is a concept with many facets. Perhaps its most common use is as a political ideal, but James's description of the nature of freedom does not begin there. His scientific training leads him to focus initially on those components of human life that are at the roots of our social conceptions of freedom. The result is that his understanding of the nature of freedom first goes back to the fundamental phenomenon of the selectivity of consciousness. In its most basic sense freedom means that we have the ability in the present to control our acts of attending to meanings, feelings, or things in the world. James regards some of these acts of attention as more free or voluntary than others. The degree of freedom or spontaneity in our attention is increased where the effort in focusing attention is felt with the greatest degrees of intensity.

James thinks that if a man can exert and control effort of this kind, these free acts of attention can have far-reaching significance. First, since James takes it to be basic that attention leads naturally to other forms of action, freedom is extended into human life as a whole. My acts of attending or thinking are in fact choices that lead me to any number of activities and projects in the world. Because there is this close relationship between paying attention, thinking, choosing, and other forms of purposeful activity, we can say that all these capacities of consciousness go together to constitute our freedom. Secondly, since consciousness is inextricably related to the world, the freedom that emanates from consciousness helps to extend freedom or novelty into the world as a whole. Novelty appears through human acts that are the results of freely chosen projects and intentions. Thus, the world that we know becomes a world of freedom.

The content of human acts depends on the mode and topic of attention in human consciousness. Morally speaking, this means that one problem to be faced is that of getting proper ideas before the mind so as to obtain desirable actions. Many conflicting topics may compete for attention. Each individual undergoes an internal struggle to determine which factors should and will take precedence in his field of consciousness, and the way he uses his freedom to focus and select from among these factors largely determines the nature and the quality of his existence. By the same token, the community is affected for good or evil by the form and content of the attention of individuals as it relates to the problems of communal existence.

For James, paying attention and thinking are moral acts. To pay attention or to think is to focus on particular interests and features of the world and at the same time to exclude other possible topics from consideration. What one attends to and how one attends are forms of action and uses of freedom that

are massive in their ethical implications. Thus, beginning with
the basic human capacity to attend to things, James's conception of freedom moves into the social and political realm. Here
it refers more directly to the structure of the social environment
in which the individual tries to develop and use the capacities
that we have been noting. In this context, freedom refers especially to an openness and a wide opportunity for thought and
action produced by a communal structure.

The freedom of consciousness that James describes points
toward a world and a human existence that is pluralistic, open-
ended, and developing. A selective, free, and finite human
consciousness that is actively related to a broad and flexible
world points to the possibility of many versions of existence.
Different life-styles and forms of meaning are the results when
these factors blend together. The world can contain many of
these versions, and no one of them can rightfully take itself
as exhaustive and final, because the world always provides
more for us to experience. At the same time, however, because
different patterns of meaning do exist and intermingle with
one another, practical social problems arise concerning how
these versions can be accommodated to one another.

At this point a spectrum of choices confronts us. At one end
of the spectrum there is the possibility of attempting to achieve
complete unity by enforcing a single view. These efforts, however, limit our freedom to think and act, and they will stifle
the human spirit. On the other end of this scale a completely
subjective and individualistic use of freedom may be advo-
cated. This plan, however, is likely to lead to an anarchy in
which a lack of unity diminishes everyone's freedom. A third
possibility is to try for a balance, a fruitful tension, between
these factors of freedom and unity. A number of particular
structures may be available for implementing this alternative,
but the goal will be the achievement of a pluralism that both
accentuates freedom and at the same time is sufficiently unified
to eliminate destructive conflicts as far as possible. These efforts will require some shared restrictions, but these will be
present for the maximum extension of the alternatives for

meaning within a world community. James is interested in the latter choice, and he recognizes that our efforts to achieve such a community must include the cultivation and the development of our capacities for choice, thought, and action, as well as attempts to build a social and political order that will allow for the creative use of these capacities.

Training and education are essential to the cultivation of our capacities. The goal, however, must not be mere indoctrination into a static way of existence. We must focus instead on the development of a humane intelligence that is inquisitive, critical, sensitive to novelty, and able to pursue a line of thought or course of action with discipline and clarity. This training will be essential to the growth and maintenance of freedom, which is the goal to be achieved if meaning in human existence is to be maximized. Education by itself, however, will not be enough. This training can reach its natural fulfillment only in a community that works to develop and perpetuate an environment in which there is a growing opportunity to use one's talents and abilities in pursuit of a meaningful way of life. This implies both the need for a structure that guarantees equal rights under law to all members of the community and the need to eliminate the narrow restrictions that accompany prejudice based on race or religious creed.

Such a society will be genuinely open, but it will obviously not be one that is totally permissive. Total permissiveness in either the individual or the community leads to disorientation, frustration, conflict and an undesirable lack of unity. These can be reduced and eliminated only if there is personal unity of purpose and communal cooperation. Doubtless there will always be lively debate and perhaps even real disagreement in the community concerning just where the particular boundary lines for conduct should be drawn, but there is little doubt that some voluntary restrictions will be needed in a community if that society is to survive. Neither an individual nor a society can be all things at the same time and still maintain its existence. Freedom and openness will have to be structured if they are not to be lost completely.

James believes that each man is entitled to seek meaning for his existence within boundaries that are established for the mutual benefit of all. Perhaps a fully meaningful life cannot be guaranteed for each man. But the human community can go far in the direction of making an environment that increases the probability that every individual can find a pattern of existence that gives his life value and dignity.

Our analysis reveals James's belief that freedom is of basic importance for human life in two main respects. First, belief in the reality of freedom is crucial if we are to regard human existence as meaningful. James sees human life as a search for meaning, but meaning is largely removed from a man's reach if we live in a world of determinism in which human activity is simply necessitated by events in the past. Freedom means the possibility of novel responses in the present, and the assumption of freedom is basic to a meaningful existence.

The second factor is a corollary of the first, namely, that if meaning is to increase, freedom must increase. James believes that the capacities to attend, think, choose, and act initially constitute our freedom. Therefore, the maximizing of freedom involves the development and growth of the capacities of consciousness. But the maximizing of freedom also involves the establishment of an environment that provides maximum opportunities for the use of our capacities and that minimizes the destructive conflicts that frustrate us. Unification of goals and purposes must accompany our freedom in both its personal and social dimensions if such an environment is to be achieved. Thus, freedom and the related factors of social and personal unity are primary values for James. They are the prerequisites for meaningful lives.

C. KNOWLEDGE AND FREEDOM

James's conviction that we live in a world of freedom also has important implications for our understanding of the nature of human knowledge, and these implications further illuminate the nature of our struggle to find meaning in our existence.

In order to bring out these points, we need to recall James's position on the relationship between consciousness and the world. In *The Principles of Psychology,* James asserts that the psychologist's understanding of the process of knowing assumes that there is an ontological difference between consciousness and its world.[32] However, this distinction does not involve a disconnection between the two. Human consciousness is always involved in a world, but this world is neither exhausted nor totally constituted by consciousness. There is always a factor of resistance and a spilling over of experience that suggests the vast scope of being which we only begin to uncover. Yet within this framework there is room for a conscious selection that does allow us to make sense of the idea that man "makes" his own world. Our knowledge of the world is one of the important factors in this process of creation.

James claims that while we know our world directly, we know it from the perspective that our particular form of consciousness allows. This perspective involves a plurality of interests that bring different versions of the world to light. In attempting to understand how this development of understanding takes place, James makes a basic distinction between two types of knowledge which he calls *knowledge of acquaintance* and *knowledge-about.*[33] James uses this distinction in two related ways. First, the distinction is his way of differentiating a level of experience consisting of sensations and feelings that are prelinguistic, pretheoretical, and prereflexive from a level of experience where there are linguistic structures, theoretical frameworks and a high degree of self-awareness. James believes that man's first encounter with the world is of the former kind and this is knowledge of acquaintance. Knowledge-about generally involves factors of the latter kind. It is a secondary level, and it is dependent knowledge of acquaintance.

Although there is structure in our initial encounter with the world at the level of acquaintance, this level of experience is also moving, ambiguous, and flexible. In order for there to be clarity and determinateness and for further development to take place, organization of our knowledge of acquaintance must take place. This is accomplished through the emergence and use of linguistic concepts and theoretical frameworks. Our knowledge of acquaintance reveals a flexible world that is malleable in terms of a plurality of conceptual frames. The particular frames that we use or try to implement all involve human choices and purposes. James believes that the linguistic concepts and theories that we develop function like sieves that we shape and dip into the stream of feeling, capturing certain components for special attention and concern. The adequacy of the frameworks that we utilize is determined by the fulfillment or the lack of fulfillment that we obtain for the expectations concerning the future that a particular conceptual structure leads us to have. Frameworks that are adequate become the cornerstones for our understanding of the world, but they are not the only ones possible, and they represent a selection from the field of possibilities.

James recognizes that for the most part the factors of experience designated by the pure forms of knowledge of acquaintance and knowledge-about are mixed up together in our lives. Thus, he employs the distinction between the two kinds of knowledge in a second way in order to refer to different perspectives of attention that are possible within a world that is already conceptually organized and permeated by self-critical thought. The difference that he is after here is simply that between a direct firsthand experience of something and an attempt to analyze and examine the thing or experience in greater detail. For example, as I engage in the act of writing, I am directly acquainted with what I am doing, but my attention is primarily focused on the content that I am trying to convey, or perhaps I am searching for the next word that I will use. This is a different sort of focus of attention than would be the case if I directed my attention primarily toward myself as I engage in the act of writing. Now I would be interested in concentrating in greater detail on factors such as how my hand moves across the page or what my particular bodily feelings are as I write. When my attention is focused in this way, James would say that I am seeking knowledge-about the act of writing with which I am already acquainted through immediate feeling.

In seeking knowledge-about I am working at a secondary level that presupposes my direct acquaintance with my own action. A basic feature of James's thought is that knowledge-about is dependent on knowledge of acquaintance. In order for there to be genuine knowledge-about, there must be knowledge of acquaintance somewhere along the line. It is true that this knowledge of acquaintance may not always be personally possessed by the one who has knowledge-about. For example, I may know something about writing without ever having written a word, but someone must have experienced writing firsthand in order for anyone to have knowledge about it.

This point clarifies the relationship between the two uses of the distinction between knowledge of acquaintance and knowledge-about. In his second use of the distinction, James recognizes that the difference between the two types of knowledge is relative. What is called knowledge-about something in one instance may be regarded as knowledge of acquaintance from another perspective and vice versa. Thus, my act of analyzing myself in the act of writing can be taken as either knowledge of acquaintance or knowledge-about, depending on the perspective that I have. But when we consider our initial encounter with the world, James maintains that there is a sharper difference between the two kinds of knowing. There is some knowledge of acquaintance that is primordial, and it is never knowledge-about in James's sense of the term, although there can be some knowledge-about it if a different perspective is assumed. This primary world of the senses, or the level of knowledge of acquaintance, is where our knowledge of the world begins, and our knowledge ultimately has reference to this level of knowledge of acquaintance, whether we are taking James's distinction in either its first or second sense.

We are "thrown" into the world in such a way that our first encounter with the world is at a level of acquaintance that leaves us with a note of ambiguity from which we can never escape. We can try to organize this experience into meaningful patterns from within, and our search for knowledge is one of our ways of doing this. However, it is clear that our freedom will make a difference to our knowledge. Working from the primal orientation that selective consciousness provides at the level of knowledge by acquaintance, we develop the ability to focus our attention and pursue our interests so that our knowledge of the world grows and develops. This means that knowing is a creative activity, and what is learned depends on the questions that we choose to ask and the methods of inquiry that we employ. These factors contribute a temporal and fallible quality to our knowledge. What we take to be established knowledge at one time may be altered in the future with respect to its status, scope, or use. Changes in our understanding of the nature and limits of Euclidean geometry or Newtonian mechanics would be examples of the point that James is making. Man is a temporal, historical being, and his capacity for knowing is included in this structure. Any knowledge that we have has a temporal factor built into it through the focus of attention that brings the knowledge into existence.

This interpretation is extended by James so as to fit certain "necessary truths" or a priori relationships in our knowledge. In the last chapter of *The Principles of Psychology*, James argues that there are necessary relations between ideas. "There is . . . no denying the fact that *the mind is filled with necessary and eternal relations which it finds between certain of its ideal conceptions, and which form a determinate system, independent of the order of frequency in which experience may have associated the conception's originals in time and space.*"[34] While accepting the reality of such relations, which may appear in mathematics, logic, and even ethics, James tries to ground them in such a way as to deny both that they are the products of a fixed, static, human nature and that they exhaustively legislate the form of our empirical experience. Instead he emphasizes the creative capacity of the mind which can develop new and original meanings that may fit together systematically and with necessity.

Existence is not exhausted in our sensory experience of it. The mind's free play can develop meanings that can influence how and what we experience via the senses, and these meanings may reveal conceptual relationships that we regard as necessary or a priori truths. These may even be put together and systematized. Some of these truths and systems, especially those of mathematics and geometry, are extremely valuable tools. But James believes that these meanings, relationships, and systems do not automatically legislate to experience. They may prove useful when applied to concrete, empirical situations, but there is no assurance about this. Man is free to try to develop relationships and systems of meaning to shape his experience, but there is no certainty that his attempts will be adequate to the reality he encounters. According to James, man may be the master of his concepts, but he is not the master of reality as a whole. Still, any success that men do have in understanding the world involves a use of freedom in focusing and clarifying concepts and meanings and in seeking to apply them in the world.

The attempt to develop conceptual frameworks that make our world and experience intelligible can result in philosophical criticism and construction, and the suggestions about knowledge that we have noted are important for James's understanding of the nature of philosophy. James believes that philosophy cannot attain the ideal of a spectatorial, objective science that will provide a final account of all being. This is because the philosopher is in and of the world, and he is influenced by his own desires and feelings. The restrictive effect of these factors can be eliminated to some extent through self-criticism, but never completely.[35] Nevertheless, insofar as philosophical inquiry meets three basic requirements it can give us some help in making our world intelligible and rational. This inquiry should (1) meet logical demands, (2) in some degree determine expectancy in regard to the future, which involves paying careful attention to facts, and (3) make a direct appeal to the powers which enable us to strive for meaning and moral value.[36] Philosophers are, of course, free to develop views that do not meet these requirements, but if these norms are not met, the philosophies in question will not exert any great influence over men.

The assumption that philosophy ought to clarify our experience without distortion or reduction is the source of the criteria that James suggests for an adequate philosophy. Logical clarity is required for efficient communication. Close attention to facts is required to avoid misleading claims. These factors are joined with the claim that an adequate philosophy will make a positive appeal to man's moral capacities and power to strive for meaning. It is the third part of the criteria that makes James's notion of philosophy different from many others. No one would deny that logical consistency is a minimal requirement for a sound philosophy, and philosophers generally claim to take account of the facts, although there may be disagreement as to what the facts are. But in the case of making positive appeals to man's powers to strive for meaning, especially when these appeals may include ethical, aesthetic, and religious dimensions, many philosophers would not agree that these factors should form any part of the criteria for an adequate philosophy. In fact, just these factors would need to be rigorously eliminated to preserve objectivity. But James's point is that it is not possible to abstract from these value factors. Our human sense of rationality includes value dimensions, and it is not likely to be satisfied by abstract appeals to objectivity that ignore these features. The value dimensions of our existence cannot be left out of our criteria for rationality if the facts are to be made humanly intelligible.

James recognizes at the same time, however, that the application of his criteria may result in a plurality of adequate philosophical theories. People may see things from different perspectives, and they may give different weight to the various factors they encounter. We may be able to rule out theories that grossly distort the facts, or that are logically inconsistent, or that totally ignore the value features of existence, but even after such criticism, we may still find that more than one view remains standing and that there is no unanimity about which view is best. This outcome is what we should expect if James's understanding of consciousness is correct. Consciousness inhabits a vast world, and each person has his way of understanding existence. The philosopher will try to take a broad overview to see how all these ideas may fit together, but even his perspective has limits. His philosophy itself will be a version, a possible understanding of being and not a final one.

In recognizing this, the philosopher can actively contribute to the extension of freedom. His criticism of dogmatic claims can prevent reduction and restriction of human life, and his constructive efforts can offer broad and unified frameworks that individuals can use in understanding their existence. If freedom is at the heart of our knowledge, it is also the case that our interest in knowledge can be for the sake of freedom. Knowledge can help us to increase our freedom and the possibilities for fulfilling the projects that we set for ourselves. James is clear that one of the important ways in which this is done is through the knowledge of our own finitude and the efforts which this knowledge stimulates for the establishment and maintenance of an open society.

D. VALUE AND FREEDOM

The idea that value largely depends on choice or freedom is another central notion in James's philosophy, and it has important ramifications for his understanding of ethical norms. James's basic point is that value or importance is determined by the selectivity of consciousness. This takes place first at the primordial level of knowledge of acquaintance, where various instincts and bodily needs may dominate. But as consciousness develops, a man gains some distance from this immediate orientation. Self-conscious choosing emerges. It can bring entirely new values into being, and it can transform and question drives, structures, and values that already exist. Ultimately, no ground for worth can be noted that is not in some way connected with man's freedom to accept or reject it. Thus, the worth of existence itself can be called into question, and James might well agree with Albert Camus's point that suicide is the primary philosophical question that a man must face.

Not only do selection and choice largely determine value, but the nature of our existence requires that our selections and choices cannot be inclusive of everything, although this might be said to be the ideal that would completely remove ethical dilemmas from our lives. In this life the individual cannot actualize all his possibilities. He must select the ones that are most important to him and drop out most of the others. This process of selection shapes the character of the individual, and the choices that he makes with respect to himself also help to determine the course of society as a whole. On the other hand, choices that the individual can make are largely set by the society, and any movement away from society's ordering will result in consequences that the individual will want to weigh carefully. Thus, the problem of how and what to choose is crucial, because of the vast range of choices that must be made and the serious consequences, both personal and communal, that follow from what one makes of himself and how he takes the world.

Man's life is a search for meaning. It is an attempt to find and to give sense to existence. Ethical reflection seeks to establish guidelines that will establish an environment where the chances for finding a meaningful pattern of life are enhanced for each individual. This reflection will be a creative process. On James's view it is clear that our determination of the content and structure of ethical principles and norms will involve choice and freedom. The norms that a man may follow do not become norms without a man's active participation in their establishment.

However, the emphasis that James places on the creative function of consciousness in structuring a moral environment must be tempered by two notes of caution. First, James is not talking about a selecting of norms that is divorced from critical reflection, and the creative use of freedom that he urges need not result in a total relativism and subjectivism. James believes that man's capacity for thought will lead him to understand that ethical reflection ought to focus on the establishment of the conditions that best foster the development of meaningful individual lives. This will lead men in the pursuit of forms of unity that will eliminate destructive conflict while at the same time keeping a high degree of freedom alive. There may be a plurality of structures that can accomplish these goals, but reasoned choosing of the sort that interests James will keep these goals in clear focus.

Secondly, James's emphasis on freedom in regard to the creation of a moral structure in the human community does not mean that ethical norms completely lack objectivity. Although they are not objective in the sense of being fixed properties of nature that merely await man's discovery, the ethical norms he has in mind are objective in the sense that they will be the result of a critical rational inquiry about structures of human existence in general and man's need for meaning in particular. In this inquiry it is recognized that man's creativity is playing a part both in the organization and weighing of the content focused upon and in the final construction of the particular norms. The latter factor means that particular statements of the normative principles may be fallible or inadequate. If this is so, revision and reconstruction will be required, and attention will need to focus again on the universal conditions necessary for maximum meaning. James believes that freedom and unity are two of the most important factors in the achievement of fully meaningful existence. In fact, it might be possible to argue that the values of freedom and unity ought to serve in a normative status as the basic ethical values to be kept in mind in our decision-making. There is a tendency in this direction in James's thought, although it never comes out explicitly. In a later chapter we will show how he might have moved in this direction.

IV

"The Moral Philosopher
and the Moral Life," 1891

DURING THE FINAL STAGES of the preparation of *The Principles of Psychology*, James also worked on ethical questions. In particular, he treated ethical problems in a series of lectures for his Harvard University students in 1888–1889. Some of the notes from these lectures still exist, and Ralph Barton Perry has reproduced important excerpts from them in *The Thought and Character of William James*. These notes are significant because they reveal a continuous stream of thought running through *The Principles of Psychology* to the essay "The Moral Philosopher and the Moral Life."

A brief consideration of these lecture notes makes a good preface to the development of the main thesis in our analysis of "The Moral Philosopher and the Moral Life." We will try to show that James's account in the essay fails to serve his own intentions adequately, because it places too much emphasis on a quantitative analysis of choosing and not enough emphasis on a qualitative view that stresses the basic values of freedom and unity. There are resources in the essay to correct this shortcoming, but James does not bring them out sufficiently. As a result, parts of his analysis may lead to unfortunate consequences. However, James's account can be helpful if it is placed in a more qualitative context, which may develop around the primary values of freedom and unity.

A. James's Lecture Notes

Four important themes stand out in the notes that Perry has reproduced. First, James suggests that, although the ethical philosopher is primarily concerned with what is good or bad, it is not possible to construct a proof of the goodness of anything in a final or presuppositionless way. Whenever we try to prove or argue for the goodness of something, we are already committed to the belief that something else is good in terms of which the object or belief in question is being judged. "To *prove* a thing good, we must conceive it as belonging to a genus already admitted good. Every ethical proof therefore involves as its major premise an ethical proposition; every argument must end in some such proposition admitted without proof."[37]

If we assume certain starting points, it follows that things will be classified as good or bad. What, then, can provide the required starting points? James believes that the selectivity of human consciousness and feeling accomplishes this task. Thus, the second basic idea that James proposes is that, insofar as any person feels a thing to be good, it is good for him. This is the source of the starting points for judging goodness. In addition, this means that there may be many different value claims in the environment, and some conflict of interest is probable. Thus, insofar as the task of the ethical philosopher is to help unify claims for goodness into a harmonious community, he faces a difficult job.

The solution to this problem would be easy if the ethical philosopher could simply actualize the abstract ideal, which would be for all claims to be fulfilled. However, this is not a likely possibility on either the social or individual levels. Our choices and our goods are frequently incompatible, and we constantly face the difficulty of deciding which goods to leave out. Since the abstract ideal is unlikely to be actualized, we must settle for a close approximation to it. The third theme, then, is James's claim that we ought to make decisions so that as many goods as possible are kept. "The solution is by Royce's 'moral insight'—consider *every* good as a real good, and *keep as many as we can.* That act is the best act which *makes for the best whole,* the best whole being that which prevails at least cost, in which the vanquished goods are least completely annulled."[38]

At this point at least two questions need to be asked about the ideas we have noted. First, is it true that all claims for goodness ought to be placed on a par, as is implied in the statements above? Secondly, does James's use of the notion of "least cost" lead to some undesirable conclusions because of its failure to give sufficient consideration to the qualities of the choices and the demands that are being made? These questions will be considered in more detail in the context of "The Moral Philosopher and the Moral Life." James's intention is to be able to give a negative answer to both of these questions, but we will see that the analysis he provides in the essay leaves him vulnerable to criticism.

The final theme in these lecture notes concerns James's view of a decision procedure for determining the resolution of conflicts that may arise when claims for goodness are made. His suggestion is that in general we should drop out all the choices that are "not organizable." The criterion for determining which choices fit into this category is established by social tradition. "No one pretends in the main to revise the decalogue, or to take up offenses against life, property, veracity, or decency into the permanent whole. If those are a man's goods, the man is not a member of the whole we mean to keep, and we sacrifice both him and his goods without a tear."[39] However, if the conflicting claims are organizable in terms of these standards, some way should be found to keep all of them in the field.

In this context James does not give a more detailed account of the distinction between goods or claims that are organizable and those that are not. It would have been helpful if he had done so, because it might have aided him in escaping from some problems that will appear more clearly in the next major section of our analysis. Nevertheless, it is important to note his belief that there can be a difference between individual goods and social goods. Although every man may have a right to claim that a given thing, action, or idea is good, this does not mean that the claim for goodness should be binding on society as a whole. The notion of goodness is ambiguous at this point. In some sense it is correct to say that anything a man claims to be good is in fact good, but it may not be unequivocally good. It may, in fact, be extremely bad if regarded from a more socially oriented perspective.

All these themes indicate that James continues to emphasize a close relationship between value and choice. Value largely rests on our choices and on our freedom. In addition, the goal of the ethical philosopher is to find a way to achieve harmony or unity among our choices, both personal and communal. This is not to be done by arbitrarily limiting freedom but by maximizing it. Freedom and unity are the values that James wishes most to protect and to extend, and they are the qualities of existence that must be kept in mind in our decisions about the priority to give to demands.

B. DEMANDS AND CONFLICTS

James's Opening Remarks and Presuppositions

At the beginning of "The Moral Philosopher and the Moral Life," James states that his main purpose is to show the impossibility of "an ethical philosophy dogmatically made up in advance."[40] There is a note of relativism in his position. James denies the view that men have access to specific moral rules that are absolute and binding for all times and places. Instead, his view is that the universe and human values are in a process of development. He takes this to mean that each existing person contributes to the character of the world and to its value.[41] Each man is entitled to hold a view about the universe and to make free choices about moral values. In fact, the nature of existence demands that we use our freedom to take a stand on questions about the nature of existence and moral values, and all of us do deal with these questions somehow, even though the decisions may not be fully articulated.

James views the ethical philosopher's task as primarily concerned with the clarification of the moral relations that will
harmonize human choices. The goal "is to find an account of
the moral relations that obtain among things, which will weave
them into the unity of a stable system, and make of the world
what one may call a genuine universe from the ethical point
of view."[42] It is crucial to see what is meant by being a harmonizer in James's view. On the one hand, unity is sought,
which involves a personal focus of purpose as well as social
cooperation. On the other hand, the goal is to extend every
individual's opportunity for free choice and fulfillment as far
as possible.

The kind of harmony that James is interested in involves a
fruitful tension between these poles. A commitment to both
freedom and unity is present, and the commitment is to create
a cooperating community in which the opportunities for free
selection and fulfillment of goals are maximized for each individual. The implication is that choices must always be exam-
ined and judged with regard to their ramifications for the
freedom and unity of the rest of the community. Thus, attention must be paid to the types or qualities of choices that men
make. If this dimension is ignored, some choices will have
the effect of arbitrarily ruling out others that deserve fulfillment.

As a harmonizer, then, the ethical philosopher has these
commitments. However, if he starts with a more specific value
claim of his own, he loses the overview that is required for
his purpose.[43] Rather than being initially interested in a single,
specific cause, the ethical philosopher should strive to order
conflicting demands by producing a decision procedure to
which all men can agree and which will help to indicate the
proper claims to keep and those to drop out. This decision procedure will consist of the application of ethical principles that
are worked out carefully in critical reflection. However, these
ethical principles must be regarded as fallible, and they will be
subject to change if their results prove undesirable.

The latter point is one of the interesting features of James's view. Ethical principles are derived from a critical examination of experience. These principles are general statements about the values and the conditions that must be given primary consideration for a full development of human life. However, because these principles are general, they may be too far removed from our particular experiences and feelings. As a result, they may allow too much or too little. If we feel that this is the case, a critical examination of both our feelings and our principles is in order, and when this is done, we may discover inadequacies in our principles. If this is the case, a revision of existing principles or a development of new ones will be required. Principles exist for man's guidance, but a man is not to be the slave of particular principles when the results that follow from them are undesirable. In "The Moral Philosopher and the Moral Life," James himself states his ethical principles in such a way that undesirable consequences can occur from their application. As a result, some revisions will be needed in his account.

The Origin of Value

If the ethical philosopher is to be successful in suggesting sound ethical principles, James believes that he must be clear about the origin of value. James tries to obtain this clarity by unpacking some of the implications that he sees surrounding the use of basic moral concepts such as "good" and "obligation." His first step is to point out that these terms have no meaning or application in a world that lacks conscious life.[44] Without some form of consciousness, there are no moral relations. His second step is to urge his reader to consider a hypothetical universe containing only one conscious being who is capable of choices. In this moral solitude the single thinker becomes a source of real goods and evils. "The moment one sentient being . . . is made a part of the universe, there is a chance for goods and evils really to exist. Moral relations now have their *status*, in that being's consciousness. So far as he feels anything to be good, he *makes* it good."[45] The emphasis that feeling something to be good makes it good is central to

James's position, although the view will ultimately lead to serious problems.

James extends his reflections on his hypothetical universe by asking whether or not truth or falsity could be ascribed to the moral judgments of the solitary thinker. His answer is that in such a situation it would not make sense to ask whether the single thinker's view of good and evil is true or not, at least in the sense of referring his views to a standard outside himself. In the case at hand the thinker is godlike. He is subject to no higher court of appeal, and his will establishes good and evil. Even in a universe with more than one thinker, the question of the truth of moral valuations does not need to arise if the thinkers never come into contact with each other so that counter-claims need to be faced. Each person would still be his own highest court of appeal. The point is that James is struck by the fact that the ethical philosopher seems to operate in a world (1) where the existing thinkers with their ideals provide the material for ethical reflection and (2) where goods and moral norms "cannot be explained by any abstract moral 'nature of things' existing antecedently to the concrete thinkers themselves with their ideals."[46]

Although James uses his hypothetical universe to describe the relations between value and a selective consciousness, he recognizes that our world is significantly different from this hypothetical universe. Instead of being a radical moral solitude, our world is communally structured and full of conflicts. In addition, one of the demands that has entered our world is that there ought to be greater harmony among our value claims and our choices. However, a problem arises at this point, namely, what is the meaning of the "ought" that the philosopher or anyone else uses in making such a claim? James's answer is similar to his account of the source of good and evil. The "ought" has to be traced back to the individual claims of an existing thinker, and beyond this one cannot go. His point is that, unless a claim is made by someone, no obligation is present. Further, James wants the analysis to work in the opposite direction as well. Not only must a claim exist for obligation to be real, but there is some obligation whenever a claim is made. "Claim and obligation are, in fact, coextensive terms; they cover each other exactly."[47]

Of course, a person will place various weights on the claims that he makes and on the obligations that he feels. In fact, rational reflection on just this question is the primary concern of ethics. At this point, however, James is merely citing the characteristics of human existence that give moral reflection its distinctive flavor, and his suggestion is that obligations require claims and that claims, simply by virtue of being made, bring with them prima facie grounds for saying that they ought to be fulfilled.

In summary, we can say that James sees the fundamental ethical categories of "good" and "obligation" as dependent on personal choices and demands. Speaking of these categories, he says, "They are objects of feeling and desire, which have no foothold or anchorage in Being, apart from the existence of actually living minds."[48] Wherever such minds exist and actualize value judgments, an ethical dimension is present in reality.

The Demand Principles

If every claim brings with it a prima facie reason for being fulfilled simply by virtue of its being made, the task of the ethical philosopher is to provide principles to help us organize the various claims and obligations that there will be in our world. Moving from the view that goodness is fundamentally related to claims or demands, James suggests that the most general and universal principle of ethical philosophy should be that the essence of goodness is the satisfaction of demands.[49] At this point James has no restrictions on the kind of demands to be considered. In fact, he suggests that the demands in question may be for anything at all. On this view, the ideal would be to fulfill every demand. However, the basic problem is that in human life our choices are frequently exclusive. Selection of one action or goal eliminates the possibility of another choice at the same time, and perhaps even at a future time. Conflict, whether internalized or set in a communal context, is an undeniable feature of human life. The result is that some demands must be left unactualized, and thus the real ethical problem is to make intelligent choices about which demands to actualize and which to drop out.[50]

As James reflects on this problem, he finds that a guiding principle emerges. "Since everything which is demanded is by that fact a good, must not the guiding principle for ethical philosophy (since all demands conjointly cannot be satisfied in this poor world) be simply to satisfy at all times *as many demands as we can?*"[51] For James, this means that a person ought to strive for a world where the least sum of dissatisfaction is awakened. However, note that the guiding principle is purely quantitative. It says that we should satisfy as many demands as possible, while at the same time frustrating as few as possible, but it makes no qualitative distinctions about the weight or priority to be given to particular demands. Note also that the guiding principle rests on the primarily quantitative principle that the essence of goodness is the simple satisfaction of demands.

Here a serious problem needs to be faced. It relates to the adequacy of James's demand principles as a decision procedure for making ethical choices. We will try to show that James's explicit statement of his demand principles leaves them inadequate, because they can too easily lead to results that would undermine faith in them. Their failure to make qualitative distinctions among demands is the ultimate reason for their inadequacy. James has the resources to provide what is needed, but he has not brought them out carefully in this context.

Resting on the view that anything that is demanded is a good, James's most general principle states that the essence of goodness is demand fulfillment. He then goes on to assert a guiding principle, namely, that we are to satisfy as many demands as possible, while at the same time frustrating as few as possible. Two examples will point out the weaknesses of these principles as they presently stand. First, conceive of a hypothetical universe consisting of four persons A, B, C, and D.

Each individual makes a demand. Both A and B demand the death of C, C demands that no one should ever be killed, and D demands that everyone should follow James's guiding ethical principle. If we couple (1) the view that fulfillment of these demands is good because anything that is demanded is a good and the essence of goodness is demand fulfillment and (2) James's guiding principle of solving conflicts by fulfilling the greatest possible number of demands and frustrating the fewest, then the death of C ought to take place. Here D's demand is not binding on all the others, but it still actively contributes to the justification of C's death. Now it seems strange, and James would agree, that a general ethical principle should allow the death of C simply because it was demanded. Other reasons ought to be involved.

Perhaps, it might be objected, C's death would not be allowed if all the individuals first subscribed to the guiding principle about demands. However, when we examine another hypothetical universe, we see that this will make no difference. Now consider individuals A, B, C, and D once again. All four make the demand that the guiding principle of James should be adhered to. In addition, we let each of them make an additional demand. A and B again demand the death of C, C demands that no one should ever be killed, and D now demands the death of C. Again the greatest demand fulfillment and the least frustration of demands will occur if C is killed.

These hypothetical examples indicate that James's principles can allow some highly questionable consequences. As his principles stand, it is possible for force of numbers to dictate what is right without any serious consideration of the qualities of the choices and demands that are being made. Even when James tries to qualify his principles further, he fails to escape this basic difficulty. Just after stating his guiding principle he says, "In the casuistic scale, therefore, those ideals must be written highest which *prevail at the least cost,* or by whose realization the least possible number of other ideals are destroyed."[52] But on James's analysis ideals depend on choices, and, if we follow his recommendation to give priority to those ideals that destroy the least possible number of other ideals, the choices that people do in fact make may still lead us to give moral justification to acts of injustice such as those noted in our illustrations above.

The problem with James's principles is that they do not have qualitative distinctions built into them from the beginning. Thus, they give him no way to distinguish demands and ideals before choices are made. Anything that is demanded is a good, and we must fulfill as many demands as possible and frustrate as few as possible. Once a demand is made, it has to be figured into the quantitative analysis. James's principles lead to one of two conclusions. Either minority claims must be given up or at least largely frustrated, or some qualitative norms must assume priority, thus calling into question the priority of James's demand principles. If the former option is selected, we might get a situation where an individual should give up his life simply because others demand it. James clearly does not want results like this. His intention is to help establish a communal structure that will maximize opportunities for self-expression for every individual and that will eliminate the narrow, capricious, and arbitrary uses of freedom that create conflicts and destroy opportunities for other men. But in order to accomplish this, the qualities of demands have to be considered at the beginning.

Taking into account his own introductory remarks and their assumptions about the primary importance of freedom and unity, James has some qualitative notions that could enrich his quantitative demand principles. Unfortunately, he fails to build these ideas into his principles. In a view that stresses freedom and unity, values can still be fundamentally dependent on human choices, and there can still be a sense in which something is good simply because it is desired. However, an orientation in terms of freedom and unity can also provide a sound moral basis for deciding in given situations that some demands should take priority over others. The test would be to decide as far and as clearly as we can whether a particular course of action will tend to extend or curtail freedom and unity, which are required and presupposed to some degree in all choices. The quantitative emphasis which is present in James's demand principles would be coupled with these values in order to help ensure their maximum extension. We would try to establish a community in which as many choices as possible would be fulfilled, but priority would be given to those that perpetuate and extend freedom and unity. These points will be developed more fully in Chapter VII. For now it is sufficient to note that some ideas in James's essay can lead to serious problems and that these problems might have been largely eliminated if he had stressed the basic assumptions with which his essay began.

Principles and Situations

Although there are basic inadequacies in the particular principles that James develops in this essay, he follows his statement of them with some comments about ethical decision-making that are fully consistent with his basic intentions. He stresses that having ethical principles is not the same as having fixed scales of values or sets of rules that are appropriate and ready-made for all situations.[53] What must be done in a specific case to achieve the highest ethical goal is largely dependent on the facts of the situation. This situational emphasis accounts for James's apparent vacillation between urging conservative and liberal positions on ethical issues. Sometimes he speaks conservatively, as, for example, when he says: "The presumption in cases of conflict must always be in favor of the conventionally recognized good. The philosopher must be a conservative, and in the construction of his casuistic scale must put the things most in accordance with the custom of the community on top."[54] This means that the philosopher must not take the wisdom of past experience too lightly. Precedents and rules forged out of previous experience must be given serious consideration. On the other hand, these factors are not absolutely binding. In some situations, James argues, the moral philosopher must take a less conservative position. Even though such action may be filled with risk and personal danger, the highest ethical life often consists in breaking communal rules and customs that have become narrow and restrictive.[55]

James stresses the fallibility and the risk of our ethical decisions. There are no absolutely fixed answers to specific ethical dilemmas. One task of ethical philosophy is to make us aware of this fact so that we can act and decide with fresh insight in each situation, rather than making each set of circumstances conform to fixed rules. On the other hand, however, this does not mean that we fail to need general guidelines that are applicable to human situations as a whole. We need general principles in order to give our decisions clarity and consistency. Without these factors sound ethical reflection does not exist.

Our ethical principles must be qualitatively oriented if they are to be helpful. The values of freedom and unity, taken as the preconditions for the pursuit and achievement of lasting meaning might be coupled with a quantitative emphasis and developed into the basic normative guideline that we need. This focus on freedom and unity would fit harmoniously with the situational emphasis that is present in James's philosophy. Keeping freedom and unity alive and growing requires both an awareness of and a sensitivity to changing trends, new facts, and human needs. Careful thinking about these particulars in the light of the general values of freedom and unity can produce good ethical decisions.

V

Belief, Openness, and Freedom

THE FIRST SECTION of this chapter focuses on two essays that James wrote between 1895–1900, and the second section deals with *The Varieties of Religious Experience*. These works fit together well for our purposes, because the themes of freedom, toleration, openness, and belief in values run through them all. The main points to be developed in the chapter are: (1) the relation of James's understanding of toleration to the value of freedom and (2) the roles of freedom and unity in his view of the relation between religion and ethics. Toleration emerges as a value that is subordinate to freedom. In addition, James's evaluation of religion, which is basically ethical in character, gives a warrant to religion as a source of extending the values of freedom and unity. He suggests that religion also retains an autonomous role that helps to assure the lasting importance of basic ethical values.

A. Essays of 1895–1900

Of the numerous essays written by James in this period, two are especially important for our study. These are "The Will to Believe" and "On a Certain Blindness in Human Beings." Working in the context of the need for choices in establishing values and patterns of meaning, both essays stress the need for our awareness of the value and meaning in human choices that may differ from our own. These essays will be helpful in our understanding of the important relationships between freedom and toleration.

"The Will to Believe," 1896

James's interest in the necessity for men to make choices in order to structure their world and his emphasis on the open-ended character of man's world and existence come together in this essay. The main thesis that James defends here is that human life is structured so that there are occasions when it is reasonable to commit oneself in spite of the fact that we lack conclusive public and objective evidence to inform us which choices are correct and which incorrect.

Some of James's colleagues argued that a man should never make a decision until objective evidence pointed conclusively in a particular direction. They used this view in order to disparage and dismiss moral and religious commitments with which they disagreed. They claimed that since these beliefs were not adequately grounded in sound evidence, they were unwarranted and should be suspended. James's essay constitutes a counterargument to this point of view. He defends a man's right to religious and moral commitments that are not totally corroborated in the public sphere. He does this because it may be necessary for us to take big risks to obtain knowledge about some aspects of our world. It may, for example, be necessary for us to move with a positive hope and trust if we are to encounter dimensions of reality such as those described in man's religions. Moreover, we may ourselves be able to move the world in the direction of our moral hopes and beliefs if we are willing to act in a situation that is ambiguous. We are ourselves factors in the final summing up concerning the moral tone of the world, and our decisions and acts influence the outcome.

James acknowledges that there are many situations that warrant holding back belief until overwhelming evidence is obtained, but there are others that can never admit of conclusive evidence until our decisions enter the field. In these cases we are called on to exercise our freedom. This may not always be an easy thing for us to do. There is risk involved in the exercise of freedom that James advocates, for there is no certainty as to what the final outcome of the decisions will be. Thus, James sees man as striving toward a future that is uncertain and vague. Human action helps to order and to give meaning to this future, and human belief is a part of this action. We have to act in faith now if we are to know in the future, and belief itself, he argues, can help us to realize our goals.

James is aware that there are some dangers in defending a person's right to believe against views that place a primary emphasis on the need to obtain conclusive evidence before committing oneself. Although he believes that these recommendations about obtaining evidence are often too conservative and that they place a higher premium on avoiding error than on finding truth, James also thinks that a radical subjectivism and a tendency to ignore the best evidence available is not a wise course of action. At one point he writes: "I quite agree that what mankind at large most lacks is criticism and caution, not faith. Its cardinal weakness is to let belief follow recklessly upon lively conception, especially when the conception has instinctive liking at its back."[56] For this reason, he tries to specify carefully the conditions under which it makes sense to take steps that outstretch the evidence that is presently available.

James recommends that a man's will should determine belief only under the following circumstances. First, a man must be faced with hypotheses (i.e., courses of action and belief) that constitute a "genuine option." In such an option the factual evidence does not point conclusively toward the correctness of either of the hypotheses in question. In addition, three other qualifications must be present for the option to be "genuine."[57] (1) The hypotheses making up the option must be living possibilities for the individual concerned, rather than being unrelated to his concrete interests and desires. (2) A decision with respect to the hypotheses must be forced instead of avoidable. (3) The decision to be made needs to be momentous, which is to say that the opportunity which elicits the decision is unique, and the decision made in that setting cannot be reversed. Cases that do not meet these qualifications are ones where we do better to wait for further evidence. For example, questions about the truth or falsity of a particular scientific hypothesis may not require our decision immediately. Further testing is possible, and more evidence can be obtained. In these cases we ought to wait for this data before making a decision.

However, we cannot always afford the luxury of waiting. Some crucial questions concerning the nature of our existence do fit the model of "genuine options." In particular, questions about the moral order and the moral direction of our world fit this structure. I may, for example, find myself faced with an option of this sort: "The values of freedom, love, and unity will become dominant in our world, or they will not." In facing these alternatives, I find that the meaning of my life is involved, and I am a factor in deciding which alternative will in fact hold. This means that there is no conclusive evidence to which I can appeal in deciding which alternative is "correct." The issue is still open, but I help to decide it with every action that I perform. The alternatives force a decision from me, and they do this in a way that is momentous, since my past can never, strictly speaking, be lived again or reversed. Thus, not only do I choose which alternative to believe without appealing to conclusive evidence, but I have the right and the responsibility to make such a choice on James's view. Opportunities to exercise our freedom are forced on us, and we are urged to accept them openly as they come and not to flee from them.

One of the things that James is urging us to see is that there is a close relationship between freedom and hope. If we live in a world that is open-ended in the way he suggests, the development of the world can be in a direction that may conform to our best human aspirations. The fact that we live as free beings in a world that is in process makes hope a legitimate and important category in human existence. At the same time, however, if hope is not to be mere wishing for the unlikely or the impossible, men must use their freedom in the direction of seeking to actualize the hopes that they possess.

Morally speaking, this means striving to bring about an environment that will match the ethical ideals that one holds.

Having emphasized the need for individual decision in specific cases, James is careful to suggest an important limitation regarding the way such beliefs should be held or lived. Beliefs that stretch beyond public evidence should be held with an awareness of their fallibility. Otherwise belief becomes irresponsible by endangering the rights of others to hold different beliefs. An openness to meanings other than our own is essential for a maximum extension of meaning in the world, and only if we are responsive to the desires and demands of others will we have an environment that is sufficiently free to make meaning possible on a broad scale. This openness must even extend to our understanding of freedom. Freedom eludes exhaustive identification with particular situations or with particular styles of life. It has a transcendence that always lures us on and that is never exhausted by what we do or say about it. Yet, if we become closed and begin to identify freedom with a particular state of affairs, we may in fact lose significant chances for the elaboration and the development of meaning in our society.

James places great stress on the importance of the freedom of the individual to seek and find a meaningful life-style of his own choosing. The very significance of life itself depends on this freedom to strive and to have a reasonable hope for success. Therefore, he suggests: "No one of us ought to issue vetoes to the other, nor should we bandy words of abuse. We ought, on the contrary, delicately and profoundly to respect one another's mental freedom: then only shall we bring about the intellectual republic; then only shall we have that spirit of inner tolerance without which all our outer tolerance is soulless, and which is empiricism's glory; then only shall we live and let live, in speculative as well as in practical things."[58]

James's plea for toleration forces consideration of another dimension of man's search for meaning. In order to be genuinely moral, toleration may require some limitations. If, for example, vetoes are never issued by us, then we may be left with an infinite toleration that is totally lacking in sound moral discrimination and that may even result in the increased control and domination of human life by forces that do not respect and foster individual freedom. Although the passage quoted above fails to put limits on toleration, James certainly does not intend to advocate this kind of infinite toleration. Rather, toleration is a value in the service of freedom and unity. It is a way of respecting the freedom of others and of shaping plural interests into a cooperative community, but toleration is not to be defended at the expense of these more primary values. If these primary values are threatened, advocates of toleration may at the same time be advocates of militant courses of action that combat the forces that undermine freedom and unity.

"On a Certain Blindness in Human Beings," 1899

The theme of toleration is approached from a different angle in "On a Certain Blindness in Human Beings." The blindness mentioned in the title of this essay stems from the fact that we are creatures with limited perspectives, especially when judgments of worth and value are made concerning other persons and their projects. As James's theories of consciousness and selfhood make clear, we naturally take a special interest in our own projects and welfare. Thus our judgments about other people are often made from a needlessly narrow bias, rather than from a perspective that tries to take account of what it would be like to live with their projects and meanings. At some time each person surely feels this lack of sensitivity in some members of his community. They do not seem to understand him clearly. They do not grasp his desires and needs, or they do not see the value and the worth of the projects that engage him. They judge him only from the perspective of meaning that they live or feel most strongly, and they never feel the qualities of his existence.

James is stressing the importance of *feeling*, or knowledge of acquaintance. Value and meaning have their roots in this level of experience. Too often we forget this, and we observe other people without trying to understand the basic feelings and the experiences that shape their lives. Then we try to make a value judgment about the life-style that we have been observing. In such cases, however, James believes: "The spectator's judgment is sure to miss the root of the matter, and to possess no truth. The subject judged knows a part of the world of reality which the judging spectator fails to see, knows more while the spectator knows less; and, wherever there is conflict of opinion and difference of vision, we are bound to believe that the truer side is the side that feels the more, and not the side that feels the less."[59]

What James means by the "truer side" needs some clarification, because his comments can be interpreted so as to make us think that spectatorial criticism is never justified. If this were true, uncriticized feeling would be the criterion of truth and value, which is an unacceptable view for him. Feeling is only a partial test of value for the ethical man, for he must never forget the social context of his life and the fact that a plurality of claims is present, which necessitates rational criticism of feeling. However, feeling is also important. Judgments concerning the value of different styles of life ought not to occur without a serious attempt to comprehend the feeling or knowledge of acquaintance that is involved.

James is urging men to become more open or phenomenological in their attempts to understand one another. The point is a simple one, but it is also frequently forgotten in our personal relations. It may not be possible to share another person's experience in a completely adequate fashion, but any attempt to pass judgment on different patterns of meaning should include an attempt to understand the feelings at the bottom of these ways of life. This is not to say that all conflict will be avoided merely by a better understanding of one another, for there may still be fundamental disagreement even with sympathetic understanding. However, some points of conflict may be removed by a more careful attempt to understand the feelings of others.

James concludes with the following comments: "And now what is the result of all these considerations and quotations? It is negative in one sense, but positive in another. It absolutely forbids us to be forward in pronouncing on the meaninglessness of forms of existence other than our own; and it commands us to tolerate, respect, and indulge those whom we see harmlessly interested and happy in their own ways, however unintelligible these may be to us. Hands off: neither the whole of truth nor the whole of good is revealed to any single observer, although each observer gains a partial superiority of insight from the peculiar position in which he stands."[60] Toleration and respect for other men involve an active concern to know their feelings, and perhaps to participate in them where possible. It is a misuse of freedom for one man to ridicule and destroy the life of another by judging and criticizing it without sensitive understanding. On the other hand, James puts some restrictions on the toleration that he calls for. It does not need to extend to those projects that sensitive understanding and critical reflection reveal to restrict the maximum possibilities for self-expression and the unity required for such activity. Toleration serves freedom and unity, but it is not to operate at their expense.

B. THE VARIETIES OF RELIGIOUS EXPERIENCE, 1902

An Ethical Evaluation of Religion

Questions about the nature and use of freedom, the qualities of unity in persons and communities, and even the relationship between one's beliefs and the toleration of those held by others are also involved in James's extensive analysis of religious phenomena in *The Varieties of Religious Experience*. James intends this work to be descriptive of many different religious phenomena, but he also evaluates and interprets them from an ethical point of view. This does not mean that James equates religion with ethics or that he tries to subsume religion under ethics. Both have an autonomy, and in the end James thinks that they can be mutually beneficial. Ethical criticism can both help to clarify religious claims and goals and give a strong warrant for religious faith if that faith produces acts that are ethically good. On the other hand, we will also see that religious faith may provide a useful grounding for ethics that cannot come from ethical reflection alone.

At the outset of his ethical evaluation of religious phenomena, James suggests that his efforts will focus on the consequences of religious faith, rather than on questions concerning its origins. It is true that there is a basic ambiguity about the religious life with respect to its origins. Is its impetus derived from the action of God in human lives, or is religious experience and feeling a purely psychological phenomenon that is unrelated to any divine powers? However, James believes that in a process of evaluation these are not the most important issues. Value depends more on a phenomenon's consequences for life as a whole. If religious phenomena produce good effects for human life, they will be of importance and positive value. On the other hand, if certain religious experiences lead to bad practical effects, that will constitute evidence favoring the view that we ought to be done with them, regardless of any supernatural sources that may be involved.[61]

James suggests that we ought to evaluate religious phenomena in terms of their "fruits for life."[62] This is an ambiguous way of speaking, and he does not specify the idea at the outset. However, by the time he completes his study, it is apparent that he does have a more specific standard which he thinks we ought to employ in making our judgments. We will see that his belief that the highest ideal for which we can strive, and in terms of which religious phenomena should be finally evaluated, is vitally related to the values of freedom and unity.

Two aspects of religious phenomena are of special importance in James's ethical evaluation of religion. The first deals with religious commitments that are fanatical. While religion can make us open to the Holy and the Transcendent, it can also become closed and narrow. This can happen, for instance, when it is claimed that a finite human demand is actually a divine demand. Whenever anything human, whether it be a

political structure, a social practice, or other belief, becomes
equated with the divine will, there may be attempts to impose
that style of life on others. Then religion may become a factor
in the limitation of human freedom and meaning. Such religious life must be criticized from an ethical point of view. In
addition, James's account of fanaticism is important because it
suggests that fanaticism is not confined to the religious life. In
fact, the qualities that James points out in this context have
been attacked frequently before. Whenever he criticizes narrowness, rigidity, dogmatism, and intolerance, he is fighting
against the traits that characterize fanaticism as described in
The Varieties of Religious Experience.

James is sympathetic to the Protestant emphasis that no
single man or group can rightfully claim more than a fallible
understanding of God. At its best the religious life retains a
basic open-endedness, and it does not become closed and rigid.
But religion is not always free of tendencies in this direction.
Individual dedication can be carried to a dangerous excess,
which James describes in the following terms: "Fanaticism
(when not a mere expression of ecclesiastical ambition) is only
loyalty carried to a convulsive extreme. When an intensely
loyal and narrow mind is one grasped by the feeling that a
certain superhuman person is worthy of its exclusive devotion,
one of the first things that happens is that it idealizes the
devotion itself."[63]

Several significant features of fanaticism can be drawn out
of this passage and its context. First, James thinks that fanaticism is a distortion of a devotion that is legitimate and
authentic. However, there is a fundamental narrowness in the
fanatic's outlook. He fails to acknowledge that experience other
than his own can have equal worth and meaning. Secondly, as
a result of his making unwarranted claims for his beliefs, he
fails to achieve a critical distance from his involvements. The
fanatic is taken over by his project or goal, rather than ordering
it himself. Thirdly, he cannot see that his own understanding
of God might fall short or at best be an approximation. He
takes his awareness of the Transcendent to be equivalent to

what is actually Transcendent, so that his devotion, ritual, and approaches to the Transcendent become inextricably linked with it. Not only is the relative made absolute, but in the fourth place, the religious fanatic will be highly sensitive to any criticism that may be directed toward his deity or religious institutions. He will regard any opposition as an enemy that must be suppressed and defeated.

We can generalize these characteristics. They involve (1) closedness to data and evidence, (2) minimized self-criticism and reflection, (3) involvement in a cause or a goal so that one is taken over by his project and absolutizes what is relative, and (4) a tendency to regard opposition as a threat and an enemy to be defeated. When we generalize in this way we can see that the qualities James is describing are not restricted to religion, but they may pervade our lives to some degree at many different levels. In fact, they seem to constitute the very style of life that James was trying to counter in the essays noted earlier in this chapter.

Freedom itself may be at the roots of a fanatical existence. The open-endedness and the lack of guarantees that accompany human freedom are not always easy to live with. Thus, we may tend to cling dogmatically to the ideas and the meanings that make us feel secure, rather than facing things as openly as we can. This is to flee from the open-endedness that freedom implies. In the religious life, freedom and open-endedness appear in the dialectic between faith and doubt that is present in every sensitive religious commitment. Although faith may bring a note of sustaining assurance with it, this assurance is not the same as absolute certainty. A religious commitment is a risk. The world could be otherwise than one's faith suggests. Insofar as the note of risk is forgotten, a man's religious commitment is a fleeing from freedom, and it will have a tendency toward narrowness and fanaticism. The authentic religious life keeps the feeling of risk alive, but the risk is coupled with a sense of fulfilled expectation. If the religious life has the qualities of fanaticism, it will be restrictive and detrimental to an open human community, which James prizes above everything else. However, if there is an openness in the religious life, it may bring basic values out into the open.

Some of these values are present in the highest form of the religious life, which James calls *saintliness*. James notes four "inner conditions" of the saintly life, and he takes these qualities to be the marks of a fully developed and authentic religious life. The qualities he notes are the following: (1) a feeling that a wider life and an ideal power exist beyond our narrow, selfish interests, (2) a sense of our friendly continuity with the ideal power, which is combined with self-surrender to its guiding influence, (3) a feeling of freedom from the limits imposed by a narrow self-interest, (4) a turning outward of the self in the direction of serving needs other than one's own.[64] These inner conditions result in practical consequences that include acts of charity and asceticism, and a process of self-purification that moves toward a playing down of self-centered motives that were once powerful in the individual's life.

James acknowledges that the practical results of the inner conditions of saintliness often produce strange, useless, and perhaps naïve practices and actions that are of questionable value even to the believers involved. On the whole, however, saintliness receives a positive evaluation from James, because it is a style of life that tends toward the growth and the perpetuation of the highest kind of community that we can conceive. These suggestions can be illustrated by focusing on his analysis of two features of saintliness that are of special importance for our purposes.

The first is asceticism, or a kind of moral heroism, which James finds to be of considerable value despite the fact that some manifestations of it have been of no social benefit. James favors asceticism because he thinks that, at its best, it is socially oriented, and it reveals a sound and a sensitive attitude toward a fundamental part of man's situation in the world. "It symbolizes . . . the belief that there is an element of real wrongness in this world, which is neither to be ignored nor evaded, but which must be squarely met and overcome by an appeal to the soul's heroic resources, and neutralized and cleansed away by suffering."[65]

It is the giving of oneself to the improvement of the human situation that justifies the ascetic life, and this is what can lead us to regard the ascetic as a moral hero. The ascetic is willing to sacrifice personal comfort and to suffer in order to serve others. While this ideal can be distorted either by becoming an ingrown set of ritual observances or by the choice of a narrow goal, asceticism has much to commend it. "The metaphysical mystery, thus recognized by common sense, that he who feeds on death that feeds on men possesses life supereminently and excellently, and meets best the secret demands of the universe, is the truth of which asceticism has been the faithful champion. The folly of the cross, so inexplicable by the intellect, has yet its indestructible vital meaning."[66]

The ascetic strives for a cause, which, broadly taken, may be said to be the elimination of evil from the world insofar as that is possible. This means that the ascetic temperament may be militant and unyielding in the face of opposition. The highest ascetic life is dedicated to the increased well-being of human life. It will work to defend, protect, and extend the interests and projects that further this cause, and it will oppose the forces that prevent the realization of this goal.

By itself, however, asceticism is not sufficient to assure a saintly life. A fanatic can be ascetic as he pursues his goal. Thus, James believes that the saintly life must combine the qualities of asceticism with those of charity, which point toward a tender and a sympathetic concern for all men. However, as was the case in his analysis of asceticism, James's view of charity is not unequivocally positive. He reminds us that the present world falls short of the ideal. This is a world full of conflict and selfishness. Regardless of its status in the ideal realm, in the present world charity and sympathy have an ambiguous position. Charity and sympathetic concern may lend comfort to powers working for ends that are destructive of value. An excess of sympathy or charity at the wrong times and places may prove harmful for society as a whole.[67] On the other hand, James also argues that the world would be a sorry place if there were no persons in it willing to be radically charitable, sympathetic, nonviolent, and even willing to take the chance of being duped rather than living in constant suspicion and hatred. The values that enter the world because of this willingness for charitable service are essential for full human life. The saintly character that manifests them does a positive service for humanity that is irreplaceable. He seeks a community in which purpose and harmony are combined.

In the highest saintly life there is a quality of tension. On the one hand, there is the desire to be charitable, sympathetic, and tender with everyone. On the other hand, the ascetic dimension of the saintly life includes the possibility that a militant stand will be required in order to eliminate the evils that produce destructive conflicts. The true saint keeps these qualities in a fruitful tension as he works for his goal, which is the establishment of a community where each man has the chance for a full development and a full use of the capacities that make him human. The charity of the saint qualifies the potential militancy of the ascetic dimension, but it is also true that the charity of the true saint is not mere permissiveness. His sympathetic understanding and tenderness will be blended with the moral firmness that the ascetic side of his saintly character reveals.

The saintly life represents a blending of several factors. If any of the factors are missing completely, especially those of asceticism and charity, the balance that constitutes the saintly life is destroyed. On the other hand, it is impossible to say in the abstract just what the exact and proper balancing of the factors ought to be in each instance. The situational structure of human existence makes saintliness a situational phenomenon as well.

James believes that the traits of saintliness are indispenable for achieving the ethical ideal. The saintly character, understood as a flexible blending of traits, can be called the highest form of human existence, because the saint is supremely fitted to live in the highest society conceivable. This James describes as follows: "It is meanwhile quite possible to conceive an imaginary society in which there should be no aggressiveness, but only sympathy and fairness—any small community of true friends now realizes such a society. Abstractly considered, such a society on a large scale would be the millennium, for every good thing might be realized there with no expense of friction."[68]

Such a society is one where freedom and unity are primary values and where these values are both maximized and properly balanced. The goods pursued in such a society depend on the use of man's freedom. On the other hand, the ideal society has "no expense of friction." Destructive conflict is not present, either at the communal or personal levels. This is the goal and the ideal that James ultimately has in mind in his evaluation of religious phenomena. A saintly character is essential if we are to approximate this ideal. The particular blending of traits making up the saintly life may need to be shifted from situation to situation, and no single blending can be regarded as absolutely the best. James is skeptical about finding a fixed, ideal character that will be ethically right for all human situations, but the qualities of saintliness are basic.

Ethics, Freedom, and God

The saintly life is the result of religious commitments. Insofar as the saintly life manifests a fruitful relationship of the traits that are necessary for the highest ethical life, both personally and communally, James suggests that on the whole religion must receive a positive evaluation.[69] This suggests that religious faith can provide a desirable grounding for the moral life. One of the ways that religious commitments do this is by providing a source of hope that our ethical goals and desires are not ultimately transient or passing, but that they are positively related to an ultimate power which is more than human. Whether or not there is such a final ground related to man's pursuit of meaning and ethical value, it is characteristic of man to seek such a ground, or at least to ask about its possibility.

The religious life is an expression of this concern. One of James's chief interests in religious phenomena is to show that the religious man acts with the faith that the transience and mutability of his existence and values may not be the final words.

James claims that belief in God can have great power in the resulting moral energy that it produces. This assertion puts him in an interesting position with respect to existential thinkers such as Sartre and Merleau-Ponty and some of the spokesmen for the contemporary "death of God" theologies. One of the themes that these men stress is that there is an incompatibility between (1) man's radical freedom and his awareness of being morally responsible to and for himself and (2) the traditional doctrines of God as a Being who is all-powerful, all-knowing, and totally self-sufficient and complete. Such a God, it is claimed, leads to a world that is already determined in every detail and where human freedom and responsibility are unreal. The traditional views of God are simply forms of determinism. Thus, in order to make sense of our experience and its feeling of radical freedom, it is recommended that man should free himself from theistic concepts.

Although James also dislikes the theological determinism that may result from some traditional conceptions of God, he does not suggest that the only solution is to eliminate theistic views completely. In fact, he believes that doing this will have the same effect as a theological determinism, namely, it will be morally debilitating. In a nontheistic humanism, death and finitude are likely to be the final words for man, and James thinks that the realization that this is so will lead to a stifling of moral energies. Thus, in several of his writings he takes a middle path. He suggests a version of theism that he thinks can call forth moral energy and give meaning to human existence.

James's suggestions point toward a pluralistic world that is in a process of development. Involved in this world, but not exhausted by it, and operating with a value perspective of his own, is a God described by James as "finite, either in power or in knowledge, or in both at once."[70] He intends these ideas to point toward the possibility of a genuine interchange between God and the world. The future is not fully determined and complete. Although God's knowledge of the possibilities for existence may be exhaustive, his knowledge of the actualities may be temporal and growing. There is room for creative novelty in the world. God and man can influence each other. They develop together, and their cooperation may lead to the establishment of a genuine moral order.

However, such a view raises an important problem. Is James's theistic framework compatible with his strong sense of human freedom? James's view of man stresses our capacities for choice and creativity and their role in our search for meaning. Particular patterns of moral order do not appear in human existence without our choices and decisions playing a major part. Man is responsible for himself. His freedom must discipline itself. Are these views compatible with a theistic structure that suggests that God has his own value orientation toward the world?

The answer is that James's sense of human freedom can be retained in a world where there is a God who has his own value orientation toward the world, provided that this orientation places a primary emphasis on freedom. Although James does not elaborate his position on these issues, we can make some brief suggestions about one way in which he might have developed this possibility. The God James has in mind places man in a world that is ambiguous and that contains vast structural possibilities. This world contains many forms of life and activity that bring new situations and new forms of being into existence. The world that we inhabit is a world of novelty and creativity. Man is free to order this world into patterns that are meaningful to him, and human morality can emerge out of this process of creativity. What might be the value perspective of God in order for all of this to be the case?

When we consider God as a creator and when we look at the vast variety and power in our world, we may imagine that freedom and unity are the primary values for God. We may regard God as the being who exercises his freedom to bring into exis-

tence and to sustain a world that is rich beyond our comprehension, both in its variety and in its creative potential, and
that is moving toward order and harmony. God seeks to combine maximum variety and freedom in the world with maximum harmony and unity, and he seeks to eliminate destructive
conflicts that lead to chaos. Such a view of God allows us to
speak of him as having a value orientation that does not negate
human freedom but rather stresses its importance. Man is
created to be free. He is free to shape and structure his world,
and God respects and values this freedom as an essential com-
ponent in his overall goal to extend creative power into the
world.

God may have general patterns or styles of existence that he
would like men to achieve as desirable components in the totality of his own creative process. But the fact that God has
these desires is not a sufficient condition to curtail man's freedom to create patterns of meaning. Freedom may retain a
priority. If human actions run contrary to the particular desires
that God has for maximizing freedom and unity, he may seek
to influence men to move in different directions. Even this,
however, can be done without destroying the sense of freedom
that James stresses. For example, God's influence on men may
take a form that is analogous to human attempts to influence
other people. One man can point out things to another person
which the latter would not otherwise notice. A man can show
another man the merits or dangers of a particular course of
action, and he can urge or even command another to act in a
particular way. Yet all of these methods of influencing others
can take place with the awareness that an individual will ultimately have to weigh the factors for himself and make his
decision in freedom. In such awareness there is a respect for a
person's freedom, and God's interaction with men may place a
premium on just this aspect of existence.

On this view God and man can help and resist each other.
There can be creative interaction and conflict between them.
God's comprehension of freedom and unity will be broader
than man's, but because God respects the freedom of presently

existing beings, the chance for support from him is likely to be increased for those projects and activities that constitute protection and extension of these qualities in the human sphere. By the same token, if man works to protect and extend freedom and unity in human life, he is likely to aid in the fulfillment of God's goals. On the other hand, God may resist projects and activities that fail to perpetuate and extend freedom and unity in human life, and if a man acts so as to curtail and destroy freedom and unity, he is likely to work at cross purposes with God.

James often suggests that one of the important things that a religious commitment does is to create a new sense of freedom in the individual. This sense of freedom unifies the self by directing it outward in service to the world which helps to create an environment conducive to full and meaningful lives. For James it could be said that an encounter with God and ethical reflection culminate in the same ideals, namely, maximized freedom and unity. The religious dimension, however, provides a foundation for ethical striving that may not be available to ethics by itself. This is the hope that human ideals may be harmoniously related to and supported by God. For James, not only is religion vindicated by an ethical analysis, but religious faith can also be a foundation for ethics, and especially for the kind of ethical life that he advocates.

VI

Pragmatism, 1906–1910

JAMES IS BEST KNOWN for his contributions to the development and the popularization of pragmatism, but not all the attention that he has received in this regard has been favorable. Some critics argue that his pragmatism is too relativistic and subjective and that it is detrimental to a sound moral perspective. In this chapter we will consider James's pragmatism, and we will see how he replies to some of these charges. We will find that his pragmatism is a broad philosophical view that stresses pluralism, freedom, and change. This means that pragmatism does not reveal any radical shift of interest in James's thinking. It is a natural and a logical extension of his earlier philosophical and psychological views. Moreover, pragmatism both reflects and supports an interest in the primacy of the ethical values of freedom and unity. James's pragmatism is relativistic, because it is situational in its thrust, but at the same time it is grounded in values that are indispensible for full human life.

A. PRAGMATISM AND MEANING

Although James is often regarded as the foremost American spokesman for pragmatism, he was not the founder of the movement. His friend Charles S. Peirce (1839–1914) first set down the basic principle of pragmatism in his paper "How to Make Our Ideas Clear," which appeared in 1878. Peirce's scientific interests focused his philosophical investigations on questions concerning methods of inquiry. One of his strong desires was to find a way to determine the meaning of scientific and philosophical concepts that would be precise and publicly oriented in its procedures and in its results. Peirce believed that there was much wasted effort and needless disagreement in our investigations because there had been little success in developing such a method. Subjective intuition, which served as the criterion for clarity, was too private and imprecise to guarantee the kind of agreement that was needed. On the other hand, if a publicly oriented procedure for obtaining clarity about the meaning of our concepts could be found, communal efforts and agreements on basic issues might be facilitated. Needless verbal disputes could be eliminated, and our inquiries and beliefs would be free of a divisive subjectivism.

Peirce's recommendation for obtaining clarity about our ideas is empirically grounded. He believes that our idea of anything is the idea of the practical effects which the thing in question will manifest. This implies that the meaning of a concept can be determined by unpacking it with respect to the practical consequences that we should expect from its object. This is clear in Peirce's basic principle: "Consider what effects, that might conceivably have practical bearings, we conceive the object of our conception to have. Then, our conception of these effects is the whole of our conception of the object."[71]

Meaning depends on the possibility of practical effects in experience, and an exhaustive accounting of these effects gives the complete meaning of the concept or idea. Consider, for example, the concept "hard." If we call an object hard, we conceive of certain practical effects concerning the object. In general, if we call an object hard, we mean that it will not be scratched by many other objects. Of course there is a relativity to the concept that will require some further specification of the expectations it will lead us to have. These specifications will be dependent on the nature of the objects in question and the context of the assertions about them. However, the con-

cept does have meaning, because there are practical consequences that it points to, and its meaning will be exhausted by
the totality of consequences that it leads us to expect.

Peirce's principle was not widely noticed until twenty years
later when James used it in an address, "Philosophical Conceptions and Practical Results," which he gave at the University
of California at Berkeley. In that address James applied
Peirce's principle to the broad metaphysical question of the
differences between theism and materialism. James's analysis
on this occasion suggests that, as far as human experience is
concerned, the main practical difference between theism and
materialism rests on the possibility of hope that the former
affords and which is largely lacking in the latter perspective.
Both conceptions account for what has happened in the past,
but the character of the future is regarded differently in the
two views. A theistic orientation offers a great degree of hope
for the achievement of the values for which men strive and for
a triumph over death and finitude.

James developed his pragmatism in the ensuing years. One
of the more elaborate expositions of his view consists of a series
of lectures on pragmatism which was published in 1907. In
this work James asserts that his version of pragmatism consists
of two parts. It is a method for the determination of meaning,
and it is also a theory about the nature of truth. As a theory of
meaning James's pragmatism continues to rely on Peirce's principle. If we are to avoid merely verbal disputes, and if we are
to settle disputes that are genuine, we need a way of obtaining
insight and agreement concerning the meaning of our concepts
and theories. James believes that the proper way to do this is
to unpack a concept or a theory with respect to the practical
consequences in our future experience that will be derived
from its object. A meaningful concept or theory will foster some
specifiable expectations in us concerning our activities in the
world. Giving a full account of those expectations will give us
the full meaning of the concept or the theory.

This approach will work for specifying the meaning of single
terms or for clarifying broad theories such as theism and ma-

terialism. Moreover, the pragmatic approach to meaning will help us to see whether or not there is any substantial difference between conflicting views. If no practical differences can be specified as following from the positions in question, then the dispute between them is merely verbal. In that case, agreement on terms should follow, and the debate should be ended. On the other hand, if there are substantial differences in the views, a specification of the concrete differences that are involved can help to shape both our future beliefs and our efforts to obtain the evidence that is required if the dispute is to be settled. The latter ideas are important because a pragmatic analysis of conflicting views will often support James's thesis in "The Will to Believe." In many questions of a religious and a moral nature, a commitment of one's life to a position is required in order to test its validity. In these cases, pragmatism will not only help to reveal the extension of hope and meaning that some of these views may provide but it will also help to show our rights to beliefs of a positive religious and moral nature. This is one of the great strengths of pragmatism in James's view. It presents an empirical orientation that is disciplined with respect to appeals for evidence, and at the same time it opens up the possibility for human beliefs and hopes that may extend beyond presently available evidence.

If we stand back from James's theory of meaning, three general features emerge. First, the method is broadly empirical. The attempts to determine meaning need to be free, open, descriptive, and nonreductive. No concept or theory is barred from consideration. Any view can be analyzed for its conceivable practical consequences. The clarity that is obtained through this process can then be used to help us pursue courses of action to attempt to verify our ideas and theories and to determine belief with respect to them. James is urging a phenomenology of meaning, which will be sensitive to the practical differences between our ideas. In an uncovering of these differences a range of possibilities for men will be clarified and opened up. The empirical thrust of James's position, then, not only implies and requires a freedom of inquiry, but it also leads to an awareness of the possibilities for meaning that we may have.

Secondly, James's analysis is future-oriented. Its emphasis is on the expectations and the future experiences that are pointed out by our concepts and our theories. This thrust fits James's basic conception of consciousness as a selecting agency that is stretched toward the future in search of new projects and goals that it can undertake and fulfill. An additional implication is that meaning may grow and develop. The past shapes the possibilities for meaning in the future, but the past has neither exhausted these possibilities nor determined them completely. Clarity about the past is indispensable for a sound understanding of the future, but in a world that is moving and developing, a man must also anticipate the future if he is to achieve lasting meaning. The pragmatic approach to meaning both reflects and supports these views.

Thirdly, James's approach to meaning has a situational and a fallibilistic character, which emerges from his long-standing idea that concepts and theories are tools or instruments for organizing our experience. As we formulate and utilize our theories and concepts, we do so from a perspective that is both finite and situated in a time and in a place. If our experience is growing, it is also limited. New experience may always overflow the conceptual boundaries that we presently use. Our awareness of future expectations is not exhaustive and complete. It is subject to error, and it will need continual revision.

These facts have ramifications for our ethical life. Ethical theories and principles themselves emerge out of a more primordial level of experience. They are the products of a selective consciousness, and although their goal is to help us achieve an environment that is ordered and harmonious, no single statement of them can be taken as absolutely final and complete. Our ethical commitments and our value perspectives may require alteration as our experience and knowledge grow and develop. A flexibility and a willingness to reexamine our positions in the light of our understanding of future outcomes takes on a basic importance. Pragmatism implies the need of perpetual criticism and reevaluation in our attempts to understand ethical concepts and theories in terms of their practical consequences. Again, the goal of this pragmatic analysis is to enable us to make sound decisions about the courses of action that will be beneficial to the development of human life.

As a method for determining the meaning of our concepts and theories, James's pragmatism is both an ethical perspective and an ethical tool. It stresses the need for a free community as the basis for inquiry and testing. It agrees to consider a wide variety of ideas and theories without initial prejudice against them. The analysis that is performed is for the sake of clarity and for the possibility of both communal openness and agreement. All these factors suggest that the pragmatic theory of meaning both reflects and supports a belief in the primary importance of freedom and unity. These values are at the heart of James's philosophy, and they will continue to be important in the second aspect of James's pragmatism, namely, his controversial theory of truth.

B. PRAGMATISM AND TRUTH

Not only do we want to know the meaning of our beliefs and theories, but we also want to know whether they are true. However, in order to have clarity about this, James suggests, the concept of truth itself ought to be analyzed pragmatically. This will help to remove ambiguities from the concept. The theory of truth that James proposes as a result of this analysis becomes a central feature of his pragmatism. It, too, is an extension of his earlier views, and it also supports his ethical orientation.

James believes that a commonsense understanding of the concept of truth rests on two basic points. First, truth is a property of some ideas or beliefs. This is an important point for James. He understands it to mean that truth and falsity do not exist if there are no ideas. There can still be states of affairs without ideas, but then there will be bare existence without truth or falsity. Secondly, true ideas "agree" with reality. This second point is one that causes difficulty. It is ambiguous, because there are different views about what is meant by an idea's "agreeing" with reality. However, James believes that this issue can be clarified if we will remember that our ideas and beliefs are essentially guides for organizing and structuring our world. They give us expectations about future experience. Therefore, this makes it natural for us to say that the truth or falsity of an idea, or its agreement or disagreement with reality, depends simply on our obtaining or failing to obtain corroboration of the expectations that follow from the idea in question. Summarizing this position, James says: *"True ideas are those that we can assimilate, validate, corroborate and verify. False ideas are those that we cannot.* That is the practical difference it makes to us to have true ideas; that, therefore, is the meaning of truth, for it is all that truth is known-as."[72] James thinks that truth *means* validation, corroboration, and verification, because that is "all that truth is known-as." The only time that we can say with accuracy that an idea or belief is true or false is when we have an idea or belief that is tested in experience so that the expectations that it gives us are either fulfilled or not fulfilled. These experiences of corroboration and verification of ideas and beliefs are at the foundation of our concept of truth, and practically speaking truth is corroboration and verification.

There are some implications of this idea that are of great importance. Man's experience and his world are continually moving and developing. Corroboration and verification are processes that are temporal and ongoing. As long as experience continues, verification is incomplete and our knowledge is fallible. This means that when we speak of the truth of an idea we must always say that it is true "insofar as" it has been verified, or that it is true "to the extent that" it has been verified. A further implication is that if corroboration and verification are temporal processes, then truth itself is also temporal. Truth is a property of ideas, and if we live in a world in which both facts and ideas are present and changing, truth may grow, develop, and change. Thus, James suggests: "The truth of an idea is not a stagnant property inherent in it. Truth *happens* to an idea. It *becomes* true, is *made* true by events."[73]

James recognizes that the latter idea will be startling to people who speak of truth as something that is absolute, eternal, and forever unchanging. James's claim, however, is that when we think in these terms we have really moved away from our empirical experiences, and we are making a broad assumption that goes beyond the particular instances of verification and corroboration that we have encountered in our temporal experience. There is no real evidence in our experience that the truth is something complete, fixed, and unchanging, although there is ample evidence that some of our ideas and beliefs have been validated and corroborated for a very long time. At best, the concept of absolute truth serves as a helpful *limit concept*. It refers to what would be the case if all the possible inquiry and experience were completed. As a limit concept, the idea of absolute truth warns us that we are not in this position, and this helps to keep us cognizant of our finitude and our fallibility.

James acknowledges that it is possible that God might have the complete awareness that would constitute absolute truth. However, as James tries to make sense of his human existence, he is not favorably disposed to this view. He finds no compelling evidence in its favor, and he thinks that the implication of such omniscience is a form of determinism which is morally debilitating. In James's view, then, we are left in a world where truth means verification. Truth, as we know it, is not something absolute and fixed, and if we think of it in these terms, we have moved to the level of an unwarranted abstraction.

James's attack on the notion that truth is absolute and fixed would have been enough to raise criticisms of his theory, but he further irritated some of his readers by his choice of language in working out his position. For instance, he sometimes equates "true" ideas with those that are "useful" or "expedient," or he suggests that the "true" idea is the idea that "works." Most people were willing to admit that if an idea were true, it would be useful or expedient. But it went too far to equate expedient and useful ideas with true ideas. Terms such as "expedient" and "useful" are too subjective and ambiguous in their meanings, and using them as synonyms for "true" will so reduce truth to the level of opinion that beliefs that are in fact false may legitimately be called true if they somehow "work" for individuals. To cite just one example, some men in other centuries believed that the earth was flat. This idea "worked" for them, and James's use of language would seem to require us to say that the idea was true. Yet we know that their belief about the flatness of the earth was false. James's theory seems to ignore the fact that some beliefs may be expedient or useful to individuals and still be false, and his theory is unacceptable for this reason. Moreover, James's language would extend a dangerous relativism into ethics. To say that the truth of ethical claims or ethical principles is inextricably related to their usefulness, expediency, or workability points toward a subjectivism that will allow men to justify any action on the basis that it is useful, expedient, or workable for them, when in fact the action in question is narrowly self-interested, detrimental to the communal good, and immoral by common standards of judgment.

James's language may leave some ambiguities that can be pushed in these directions, but he does attempt to specify his theory of truth to avoid a destructive subjectivism and relativism. We can bring out these points by considering the following passage from *Pragmatism*: "'The true,' to put it very briefly, is only the expedient in the way of our thinking, just as 'the right' is only the expedient in the way of our behaving. Expedient in almost any fashion; and expedient in the long run and on the whole of course; for what meets expediently all the experience in sight won't necessarily meet all farther experiences equally satisfactorily. Experience, as we know, has ways of *boiling over,* and making us correct our present formulas."[74] Here James connects the idea of expediency with the qualifications "in the long run" and "on the whole." Admittedly these are general ideas, but if they are understood in the whole context of James's philosophy, they are more substantial. In particular, we will see that both of the qualifications fit with his ethical views.

When James says that the truth of a belief or a theory depends on its being expedient over "the long run" and "on the whole," he is emphasizing the importance of repeated testing and verification of our ideas plus the need for consistency and coherence among all of our beliefs and theories. These are communally oriented qualifications that deny the appropriateness of a narrowly subjective interpretation of "expediency" and "usefulness." James takes it for granted that it is foolish to act without evaluating and testing our beliefs as widely and as critically as possible. We will have lasting truth and we will minimize narrowness and error only if we do test and evaluate in this way. Of course, no person is forced to follow this course of action. Our freedom makes it possible for us to act irrationally and narrowly. A person can act and think with very little criticism and testing, and he can interpret the notion of expediency in a radically subjective fashion. However, if he does so, there is little chance that repeated experience will support his claims for truth.

These suggestions also aid James in developing a reply to the critics who attack his equation of expediency, usefulness, workability and truth on the grounds that his theory too quickly passes over the fact that an idea can work for someone and still be false. James stresses two points. First, a given belief may have many practical consequences and implications. We may not be completely aware of all of these possibilities, and we may not have verification of some that we are aware of. Secondly, our beliefs are always in a process of receiving or failing to receive verification of the many consequences that they involve. We never possess truth that is complete or absolute. We may be inclined to regard partial verification of beliefs or theories as complete verification, but there is always the possibility that experience will lead us to change our minds. For example this is what has happened to the belief about the flatness of the earth. Men found that some of the expectations fostered by this belief received verification, and they came to regard the belief as holding good with respect to all the expectations that it legitimately fostered in them. However, later experience shows that the belief is not valid for all of the expectations that it creates. If regarded as holding for all these expectations, the idea is in fact false. We will not receive verification of all the expectations that it leads us to have.

Nevertheless, although some beliefs may not hold for all the expectations that they foster, and hence are false if regarded from that perspective, they may still have a limited usefulness and a limited truth. James's pragmatism means that a belief is true insofar as the expectations it fosters are corroborated. On this basis, we can take our example of a belief about the flatness of the earth and say that it is partly or relatively true. Taking the earth in this way may work very well in certain types of our actions, and if we can specify the context sufficiently, it will make perfectly good sense to say that the earth is flat.

These views suggest that there is a sense in which a belief can be false from one perspective and still be expedient, useful, and true from another. But James does not believe that a belief can be both expedient or useful and totally false at the same time. The very definition of a belief's or an idea's expediency and truth is that it gives us some expectations that get fulfilled. If an idea does this, it is true to that extent, but an idea that gives us expectations that our experience never fulfills will not be true in any respect. The charge that James's theory is confused because it too quickly passes over the fact that a belief can work and still be false is answered by James in a way that takes account of certain subtle features of our language and our experience that his critics ignore. James's pragmatism focuses our attention on the fact that a proposition may point to many different practical consequences. He regards a proposition as true insofar as we can verify the expectations it creates in us, and in other cases he regards the proposition as false.

But the crux of the matter always revolves around obtaining public and personal evidence for our beliefs so that we will obtain consistency and coherence in our thoughts and actions.

James is clear that the wise course of action is to pursue a policy of critical testing of our beliefs. Even then, human existence is filled with many risks, because our testing will be finite and fallible. This line of thought extends into the ethical sphere as well. A person who chooses in total isolation from the insights of critical reflection concerning basic communal values has little chance of finding full meaning and success for his projects. He may, in fact, undercut the very freedom and unity that are needed for meaning and success. When ethical considerations are involved, we will also need to know and test in accordance with what is expedient in the long run and on the whole. These considerations will point us toward the establishment of an environment that will maximize our chances for free expression and the creation of meaning. Acts that seek to extend and to protect those qualities will be the ones that are genuinely expedient and useful to men.

The truth and falsity of moral beliefs will be inextricably bound up with our evaluation of the degree to which the consequences they produce will be conducive to the establishment of an environment in which meaning and free expression will flourish. This will indicate a need for flexibility in our moral reflection. Our goal of an environment that allows for maximum meaning and free expression may necessitate criticism and alteration of established practices and rules for conduct. Sensitivity to changing circumstances and desires will require fresh and creative decisions about how to establish the environment that we need. Even our statement of basic moral principles will need to be reexamined for increased clarity and guidance as our understanding of human existence develops. Thus, in a world of change, a certain degree of relativism is essential to the ethical life. But this does not need to result in a radical individualism and subjectivism that ignores the need for communal cooperation and normative guidelines. As we seek for meaning, there are conditions that we all require if there is to be a chance for widespread success. It is expedient to work for these ends and to give them priority in our lives. James's theory does not rule out the possibility that a person may act with a narrow notion of expediency in making his ethical choices. No theory can rule out that possibility. But James clearly rules this out as a proper reading of his theory of truth with respect to ethical values and principles.

As was the case with James's pragmatic test for meaning, his pragmatic theory of truth both reflects and supports his interest in the basic values of freedom and unity. Truth is obtained only through open inquiry in a free community. Obtaining truth will depend on communal cooperation and personal integrity. On the other hand, freedom depends on knowledge and truth. An increase in knowledge and truth will give us the possibility of greater success in our projects and more options from which to pick. This makes it imperative that we have unified and creative efforts to obtain more understanding about the world that we inhabit. Finally, the pragmatic approach is intended to aid us in the settlement of disputes about the truth of various claims that we may make. If we seek empirical verification and a harmonious relationship among the beliefs that we hold, greater unity will be the result.

James's pragmatism points toward the need to protect and extend freedom and unity in a pluralistic setting. His theory is grounded in basic ethical values. It is calculated both to clarify aspects of our existential predicament and to offer some guidance for the shaping of a world that will allow for the free pursuit of meaning and the achicvement of unified individuals and communities.

VII

Freedom, Unity, and Norms

THE PRIMARY GOAL of our study thus far has been to indicate the values that are at the center of James's ethical perspective. Freedom and unity have emerged in this role because of their importance as prerequisites for the pursuit and the achievement of lasting meaning. This chapter will extend James's perspective in two ways. First, we will want to see what norm or principle will take priority in guiding our decisions in accord with these values. Secondly, we will want to see what the nature of this norm will be. Here it is important to note that a value is not the same thing as a principle or a norm. A principle or a norm is a statement that directs our thoughts and our actions toward the preservation and extension of values in human life. James gives some clues about how the values of freedom and unity might be incorporated into a norm or a principle, but he does not speak explicitly on this point. We will try to develop one approach that he might have taken in working out this aspect of his ethics. We will move beyond his explicit statements, but our suggestions will be in harmony with those statements and with the general tone of his entire philosophy.

If we can clarify how James might have developed his ideas about the relation of freedom and unity to ethical norms, it will then be possible in the next chapter to shed further light on two closely related problems with which he did grapple. These issues are the questions of how value beliefs ought to be held, and what the proper extent and nature of toleration should be concerning beliefs that are different from or in conflict with our own. Again, the treatment of these problems will move beyond James's explicitly stated views, but the suggestions will be consistent with his position.

The present chapter has two sections. First, a review of some of the basic features of James's views concerning freedom and unity will clarify the foundational status of these values and lay the groundwork for insight about the basic ethical norm that we will propose. The second section will make some suggestions about the kind of ethical norm that it is possible to have in James's ethical perspective. It will also give an outline of the ethical norm that should take priority in our attempts to make sound ethical decisions.

A. The Foundational Status of Freedom and Unity

In *The Principles of Psychology*, freedom is closely related to consciousness. Selective consciousness is the source of freedom, and freedom pervades our whole life through our ability to concentrate on ideas and projects. This aspect of James's view of freedom focuses primarily on the capacities that we have for thought, choice, and action. James does not offer indubitable proof of the freedom of these capacities. However, he argues that the question is open from an objective point of view and that the individual has a legitimate right to believe that he is a free and original source of activity and meaning. In fact, James regards a belief in this freedom as essential to the development of meaning.

Freedom initially consists of our capacities to attend to the development of goals and projects, but James always connects this idea with the view that men should be able to fulfill these goals and projects as far as possible. Freedom must extend to the fulfillment of our goals and projects. This view stems from James's belief that value is dependent on choice and selection. If a choice is made, this makes the object of the choice a good, and a prima facie ground for fulfillment is established. However, the fact that choices may conflict leads to the necessity for principles to help us decide which goals and projects ought to have priority. This is in turn necessitates focusing our attention on those conditions and values which are of primary importance in the fulfillment of choices. The projects and the goals that are in accord with those conditions and that help to extend them are the natural candidates for priority.

James cited the need for ethical principles in "The Moral Philosopher and the Moral Life." In that essay he suggested that we should follow the principle of fulfilling as many demands as possible while at the same time frustrating as few demands as possible. This principle rested on the additional principle that the basic good was demand fulfillment and on the view that anything that was demanded was by virtue of that fact, a good to be fulfilled. This analysis, however, proved to be susceptible to interpretations that could lead to undesirable consequences. Nevertheless these problems could have been overcome if James had placed his essentially quantitative analysis in a position subordinate to the values of freedom and unity. Showing how this relationship is possible helps to clarify the foundational status of freedom and unity.

The first factor to notice is James's claim in "The Moral Philosopher and the Moral Life" that if a thing or a goal is desired, this makes it good and fulfillment is called for. We have seen that James's development of this idea has limitations and that it can lead to undesirable results, since it does not allow sufficient qualitative distinctions. However, the needed qualitative distinctions are implied in the very acts of choosing and obtaining fulfillment. Choosing and fulfillment depend on freedom. What will be valuable to us and what will make our lives meaningful depend on a use of freedom. Freedom qualifies as a fundamental value, because it grounds all the values and the meanings that we can develop. It is even the precondition for choosing itself as a primary value. This latter fact is crucial, because when freedom chooses itself, we have pushed back as far as we can. We are at the foundations of meaningful human existence and value. Our tendency may be to take freedom for granted because it is foundational, but it is in fact the basic value that must be preserved and extended if projects are to be pursued and if meaning is to be found. The destruction of freedom will be coupled with the elimination of meaning.

The character that this foundational freedom must have, if meaning is to be obtained, is shaped in part by the fact that our present world is one in which conflicts occur. This world is not the ideal one where all demands are fulfilled without frustration. However, the ideal world and the actual world do share some important features. In both, what is good depends on the exercise of freedom, and a maximum amount of goodness is desirable. Maximizing goodness will depend on a maximum use and extension of freedom.

Moreover, maximum use and extension of freedom require the development of personal and social unity. To use freedom successfully, a man must be able to fit things together into a pattern. This requires gaining some distance from his immediate situation and the development of an overarching perspective and goal. Otherwise one's choices are likely to cancel each other out, resulting in personal disintegration and the loss of meaning. One of the most important factors to be considered in achieving an overarching perspective is the fact that we live in a communal setting. My life, freedom, and goals cannot be isolated from other men. If my society is torn by war, hatred, poverty, or prejudice, my existence and interests are influenced and threatened, and the chances for fulfillment are minimized. Thus, my freedom and meaning will be reduced unless my actions work for the well-being of society as a whole. Social unity or harmony needs to go together with the personal unity that must be present for a fruitful use of freedom. In fact, it is in service to the community that one may find the meaning that he seeks.

Freedom and unity go together as the prerequisites for obtaining fulfillment and lasting meaning. The extent to which these values are maximized will determine the extent to which meaning may be found and fulfillment achieved for the goals of individuals. It is important to note that there is a quantitative qualification in this analysis and that it is related to the values of freedom and unity. James has a quantitative emphasis in his demand principles in "The Moral Philosopher and the Moral Life." But he does not give sufficient stress to the fact that the conditions for the maximum fulfillment of demands involve the maximum extension of freedom and unity. If his account is to be ethically sound, the quantitative emphasis must be in the service of these fundamental qualities. To avoid needless restrictions we will want to fulfill as many choices as possible and frustrate as few as possible, but now the quantitative emphasis will give priority to those demands and goals that serve to support and maximize freedom and unity. Demands that do not work in this direction may rightfully be frustrated.

The quantitative qualification urges us to extend opportunities for choice and fulfillment as far as possible. This will place some difficult demands on us, because it eliminates the possibility of moral justification for an outlook that is narrow and self-centered. Care and concern about freedom and unity and the fulfillment of choices may be relatively easy when confined to one's own interests or to the circle of one's family and friends. However, when we are urged to extend our concern far beyond these dimensions, as we surely are, then the responsibilities that face a man may become harder to fulfill. The ethical position that can be derived from James's view may judge us harshly. It is unlikely that any person has done as much as he could to extend freedom and unity in our world. Insofar as this is the case, each man is guilty before others.

If we are to approximate the ideal world in which there are no destructive conflicts between persons, people will need to pursue their interests without arbitrarily limiting those of others. Moreover, there will need to be a great emphasis on the importance of helping and encouraging others. A freedom that stops with man's ability to think of possibilities is inadequate. James's notion of freedom and unity stresses the need for positive efforts to build an environment in which the chances for obtaining fulfillment are broadly extended. His view reflects and supports the belief that communal cooperation can and ought to increase the freedom and the opportunity for individuals. This cooperation can provide an environment that both stimulates our capacities for thought, choice, and action and that lures our energies on by increasing the possibilities for success in fulfilling the choices that we make.

The development of such an environment requires people to think very carefully about the qualities of their choices. This places a premium on an educational process that stresses the inextricable relations between individual and communal wellbeing. People will need to learn to judge their demands from a broad social perspective before they act on them. If they fail to do this, freedom will be used capriciously, and it may be destroyed. On the other hand, critical evaluation of one's choices can protect and extend freedom, and at the same time this kind of thinking will both reflect and support the ideals of personal and social unity. Critical evaluation of choices and demands will lead to a clarification of personal purpose, and it may also increase one's awareness of his relation to society as a whole. The use of freedom that results will then be likely to concentrate on the establishment of a community where each person finds many opportunities for himself and contributes to the opportunities for others.

B. An Existential Norm

The development of the kind of environment described above can be facilitated if we have a basic norm or principle that will focus our attention efficiently on the factors that need to be given primary consideration. It is possible to obtain such a norm in James's ethics, but before stating it, we need to clarify the nature such a norm would have in this context.

James's ethics stresses the view that meaning does not appear in our existence without man's freedom and creativity playing a part. This does not mean, however, that man's choices are the only significant factors. James is aware that human existence has universal structures that are not dependent on our choices and desires. For example, communal life, the exclusive character of choosing, and basic physiological needs are factors of this sort. Furthermore, no man is consulted about his birth, his initial bodily structure, or even many of the situations in which he finds himself. Self-conscious willing and choosing always take place within structures of these kinds. These structures constitute the boundaries within which we exist.

Nevertheless, it is the case that our choices and desires do interact with these structures. The particular meaning that these structures have is dependent in part on my choices and reactions concerning them. For example, if I have certain physical disabilities from birth, their particular meaning is partly dependent on the desires or the goals that I would like to fulfill. This fact exemplifies James's belief that there is a flexibility in my existence and my world that corresponds with my capacities for freedom. I help to make the world's meaning by my interaction with the forms of being that I encounter. My existence and my world have no single meaning that I must either discover and accept or else be in error. Meaning grows and develops with my freedom.

If I am to make sense of my world and my existence in an ordered fashion, I must make choices and exercise my freedom. This is a basic part of being human. But these choices must be coupled with an understanding of the possibilities and the consequences that face me as I choose. My existence and my world are not infinitely flexible. I will encounter resistance and frustration if I fail to take basic structures into account. James urges a style of life that brings all of a man's powers together harmoniously. He realizes that life is stretched out toward a future where intelligent choices must be made in order for meaning to exist.

The development of fruitful meanings for centering our existence entails a dialectical interaction between choice and understanding. If we pursue this point, we will note that ethical norms are essential factors in our pursuit for meaning, and as such, they are not isolated from our decisions and choices. On the other hand, if a norm is to be both rational and authoritative, it must not rest merely on human choices. If the latter situation occurs, it may result in an extreme relativism, which is precisely what James wants to avoid if possible. The question, then, is whether there are norms that can be found that will recognize the fundamental role of choice without accenting it to an extreme. The type of norm required would consider the role of human choice where basic meanings are concerned, but it would temper this with the view that reasoned choices must take account of other basic facts of human existence. As we will now try to show, James could have argued that freedom and unity can have a normative status that meets these requirements.

The values of freedom and unity could be combined into what has recently been called an *existential norm*.[75] The idea of an existential norm has been developed in an attempt to cut against two long-standing tendencies in ethics. On the one hand, there is an objectivism that stresses the idea that man possesses a fixed nature that is related to an objective ordering of values and norms that is independent of man's choosing for its status, meaning, and content. On this view, man's task is essentially to discover what is already present in his existence and his world. Little emphasis is placed either on the possibility that there are ambiguities in existence itself, or on the crucial part that man's freedom plays in creating and ordering values in meaningful patterns for his own life. While it is true that James retains the idea that there are basic structures to our existence which are not fully dependent on our freedom, he denies the view that ethical values and norms are independent of our freedom. Man's free consciousness, working within its world, is a basic factor in the determination of ethical values and norms. What a man will and ought to become and what he will and ought to value are not totally fixed in the natural order, but are partly dependent on the workings of selection and self-understanding at both the individual and the social levels. Values and norms have their place in the natural order, but they are not present apart from man's active work in selecting and creating them.

On the other hand, there has been and continues to be a tradition in ethics that emphasizes the subjective or the emotive side in an interpretation of values and norms. Here the stress is on the fact that ethical valuations are primarily expressions of personal feeling or emotion. If it is pushed very far, such an emphasis can remove ethical questions and disputes from the sphere of rational discussion. If everything is to rest on feeling, and one man's feeling is taken to be as good as another's, we are on the way to a radical subjectivism and relativism. At times James seems to be closely allied with such a perspective. This is especially true in "The Moral Philosopher and the Moral Life," where it appears that something is good simply because someone demands it or likes it. However, we have seen that there is another strand in his thought that cuts against this emotivism. Basic structures of human life and the character of choosing itself, including its foundations and their value, are emphasized here. This emphasis brings out the primary importance of freedom and unity, and the status these values receive is not due to arbitrary choosing.

An existential norm both incorporates and rejects some features represented in the extremes we have noted. The content of an existential norm comes from a careful analysis of the structure of human existence. This includes cognizance of the fact that men are beings who choose and create and who consciously seek meaning for their existence. The world is the field in which this venture takes place, but it is both ambiguous and flexible. The possibilities for meaning are plural, and they can, in fact, be extended and developed through man's efforts to shape his environment and develop his own potentialities.

In order for meaning to be found, developed, and extended, certain conditions are of fundamental importance. We have seen that the basic ones that James stresses are freedom and unity. Unless these values are in a position of priority, the chances for an ordered and meaningful existence are minimal. The ethical philosopher, who is concerned with the preservation and extension of basic values, needs to formulate ethical principles that will call attention to these values and that will help us in making sound decisions. Man's freedom is also at work in this creative process. The critical use of reason in ethical analysis is itself a project that a man engages in through his free choice. The particular facts of existence that are focused upon and the weight that is given to the factors constitute a pattern of meaning that involves a free and creative use of reason. The process is not simply the passive receiving of a single, fixed picture of reality. Further, the establishment of particular principles as normative and the willingness to adhere to them also constitute acts of freedom. In fact, at this point, freedom is disciplining itself. This discipline that freedom imposes on itself is not based on an uncritical fiat, but on a reasoned analysis of the conditions that men universally require in order to obtain meaning. Understanding and choice are bound up together on all these levels, and the idea of an existential norm captures this fact.

James could argue that freedom and unity combine to form the basic existential norm. We have already noted that freedom and unity are of primary value, and this position leads to their normative status. When we look to see what stands at the foundation of all the projects and the meanings that we try to develop, we find freedom. Freedom calls for primary concern, respect, and maximum extension. We take it over or appropriate it for a normative use. The result is that judgments concerning the worth of an action will concentrate on the degree to which an action extends or curtails this basic freedom.

At the same time the emphasis on freedom has implications for our value of unity. If freedom is to be extended, it must discipline itself both personally and communally. On the personal level this means developing a unity of purpose so that choosing and action are harmonious for the self. This also involves a communal awareness and concern, for the individual is a part of society. A communal awareness can regulate freedom and prevent its use from being narrow and selfish. Thus, unity has normative features in conjunction with freedom. It, too, presents itself as something worthy of pursuit and protection. It can also be chosen for a normative status with the result that judgments concerning the worth of an action will also concentrate on the degree of unity that it produces.

Putting these factors together, we could say that the primary existential norm is: *Act so as to maximize freedom and unity.* This norm tells us that freedom and unity are the basic values that stand at the foundation of meaning. Both must be maximized to provide an environment that is conducive to obtaining meaning. To do this, a tension must be kept between the two factors. If freedom is stressed at the expense of unity, chaos and frustration may appear. If unity is stressed at the expense of freedom, a beneficial variety and richness in existence may be lost.

Of course no man or society is absolutely required to maintain this norm in a position of priority. If this were true, freedom would not be real. The discipline that is called for must come as an act of freedom itself. On the other hand, if this priority is not maintained, there will be a basic sanction imposed on both individual and communal life. This sanction will be constituted by a loss of meaning and orientation. Maximum freedom and unity must be present for meaning to be full. Wherever there is emptiness or a feeling of the loss of meaning, the chances are good that at some point value priorities concerning freedom and unity have been misplaced.

An individual can experience a loss of meaning through his own misuse of freedom, or he may experience feelings of emptiness and meaninglessness as the result of the actions of a society that is closed to his interests and his needs. In either case the society itself is also likely to suffer, but this is especially likely to occur in situations of the latter kind. A society that is essentially closed to the interests and needs of some of its members will lose the enthusiastic cooperation of those who find themselves pushed out of the mainstream of the community. In fact, a community that is narrow in its extension of opportunity may find some of its members so frustrated that they will find meaning only in desperate attempts to change society by disruption and perhaps even violence. The best safeguard that can be taken against such action is to extend freedom and unity for all the members of the community.

Now we need to examine another problem in more detail. How will this basic existential norm help us in making concrete decisions? The first point to note is that this norm is not a rule. It does not tell us specifically to do one thing or another without further reflection. In fact, the basic function of a norm such as this is to call our attention to factors of primary importance that we must think about and reflect on in relation to the concrete circumstances and problems that we face. One of the points that James made in *The Principles of Psychology* is that a chief task in ethics is to get men to concentrate on the right things. An ethical norm or principle serves in this way. It helps us to attend to the factors that must be given primary consideration if our lives and communities are to achieve their full potential.

The statement, "Act so as to maximize freedom and unity," is actually a "trigger phrase" that should stimulate reflection about human existence as a whole. Using this existential norm in making decisions requires some understanding of the structure of existence in which this norm is rooted. The norm is pointing toward conditions that must be protected and extended in order for there to be meaning in existence. Before the norm will be of help, however, one must understand why those conditions must be protected and extended and what man's situation is as he tries to achieve meaning.

This points to one of the major differences between a norm and a rule. A rule can be obeyed without one's understanding why it exists or what exactly it is intended to accomplish, but a principle is not helpful unless it is accompanied by understanding of its foundations and its purposes. If this understanding accompanies the norm, it can serve as an efficient way to focus our attention on the basic values at stake as we try to make sound decisions that are tailored for the circumstances and the problems in question.

As we concentrate on basic conditions, our existential norm will aid us in two ways. First, it will help us to see how we can balance the interests, desires, and proposals for action that are already before us. Our norm will help us to make judgments about the quality and the organization of these factors. To make these judgments and to assign priorities for our projects, we will seek to understand how the proposed courses of action will extend or curtail our opportunities for choice and fulfillment. We will also try to see the effects of choices with respect to personal and communal unity. The autonomy of individuals will be respected in this analysis, but always with the care to show that this autonomy needs to operate for the community and in the direction of a unifying personal focus of meaning. In all cases, priority will be given to actions that maximize freedom and unity, and reflection about priorities will require flexibility and imagination, because working to maximize freedom and unity will mean doing different things at different times.

Imagination is also at the roots of the second task that our existential norm can help us to perform. Imaginative thought that focuses on the values of freedom and unity may lead us to formulate new projects and goals that will transform the environment and existing interests that are too narrow. Our norm is future-oriented in the sense that it urges us to seek out new ways of living and acting beyond present circumstances and choices. It urges us to seek fresh courses of action that will be conducive to new extensions of freedom and unity. However, it must also be remembered that imagination will not culminate in good decisions if it is isolated from particular facts. Good decisions cannot be made without a careful situational analysis. This analysis will need to combine consideration of the precedents and rules set by past experience, careful understanding of present circumstances, and imaginative calculation of future possibilities and outcomes.

James believes that the primary task of the ethical philosopher is to draw out basic principles which will guide our reflection as we seek creative decisions for particular situations. The existential norm that we have suggested will direct our attention in the right way. It emphasizes the primacy of the values of freedom and unity, and it requires us to analyze situations with great care in order to implement these values. However, the existential norm will not eliminate all of the ambiguities from our existence. Our vision into the future is always finite. We can never be sure that needless prejudice and bias do not influence our decisions. We can never be sure that we have weighed the facts as carefully as we should. In other words, using our norm does not always mean that we will make good decisions. On the other hand, good ethical decisions rarely occur by chance. They are generally the result of reflection in terms of norms that are grounded in a critical understanding of man's situation. James's philosophy implies a basic norm which can help us. Although an appeal to it is not a sufficient condition for good ethical decisions, such an appeal is a necessary condition for the establishment of an environment in which meaning and value can flourish.

VIII

Devotion and Toleration

IN THE LAST CHAPTER we discussed the normative status that can be granted to the values of freedom and unity in James's ethics. Freedom and unity serve as primary values, because they are the fundamental conditions for the creation of lasting meanings. In order for meaning to be extended, freedom and unity need to be maximized. When combined, these values form the primary norm for guiding our decisions. It states that we should act so as to maximize freedom and unity. This norm operates in our attempts to interpret and clarify the confusing details of our lives. It guides our reflection, but it does not give us ready-made solutions to problems. A situational approach is always needed to determine what ought to be done to organize human desires and needs and to extend freedom and unity in a particular set of circumstances. This means that there is always the risk that our choices may not be the best, but we must act with as much foresight as we can gain, trying to clarify ambiguity and keeping an openness to the future that precludes rigidity and dogmatic judgments. James's position is a form of relativism. However, this relativism is desirable, and it is based on a fundamental norm that provides the guidelines for decision-making.

The present chapter will develop these ideas further by accenting two manifestations of freedom and unity, namely, devotion to goals and ideals and toleration. These aspects of freedom and unity are important, because they are involved in James's position on the individual's relation to the community. Devotion, as we shall see, places a primary emphasis on the individual's need to develop meanings and values that direct his conduct. Toleration, on the other hand, places a greater emphasis on communal cooperation and the minimizing of conflicts where individual choices differ. Devotion and toleration should not be isolated from each other. James's view of freedom and unity requires them to go together, and the form that this relation takes is largely determined by the primordial values of freedom and unity.

A. Devotion

James defends the right of the individual to dedicate himself to a cause or a goal. Each person needs to find a basic meaning that can orient his life, and he needs goals that he can pursue with courage, honesty, and seriousness. "The solid meaning of life is always the same eternal thing,—the marriage, namely, of some unhabitual ideal, however special, with some fidelity, courage, and endurance; with some man's or woman's pains.— And, whatever or wherever life may be, there will always be the chance for that marriage to take place."[76] The idea of devotion is central in James's arguments for the legitimacy of commitments to goals, including those that are moral and religious. However, it is natural to ask *how* these beliefs, goals, or desires are to be held or lived, because it is clear that overzealous adherence to them may destroy the rights of others and lead to chaos and the destruction of value.

James was aware of this problem. This is revealed in his frequent pleas for the toleration of others and in his brief analysis of religious fanaticism in *The Varieties of Religious Experience*. He was convinced that commitment and devotion did not need to be closed and narrow. A comparison of the characteristics of a genuine life of devotion with those of a fanatical life will help us to specify the character of the devoted life, and this comparison will also reveal substantial differences in the two life-styles. We can begin by recalling some of the insights about fanaticism noted in *The Varieties of Religious Experience*. In that work James focused primarily on the manifestations of fanaticism in religion. Yet the qualities of life that he points out are not restricted to religious commitments. They can permeate life as a whole.

James's discussion in *The Varieties of Religious Experience* suggests that there are four basic factors in the fanatical style of life. First, this life-style is closed and narrow in its respect for and willingness to seek out new data. It is doctrinaire, dogmatic, and generally closed to the claims of others, especially when these stand in opposition to one's own. When confronted with differing claims, the fanatic may, for example, dismiss them without an open and a critical examination by branding them as the products of a deluded mind or a political conspiracy. Secondly, the fanatic minimizes self-criticism and reflection about the basic status of his primary beliefs and allegiances. A person with fanatical tendencies may be highly self-critical of his progress in achieving his goal, but he rarely questions or wonders about the status of the goal he pursues. If such questions arise, they need to be quickly silenced, because they may reveal a wavering of commitment.

This points out a third feature of fanaticism. The fanatic absolutizes the relative. He is involved with his goal or belief so that he is taken over by it. He is unable or unwilling to gain a sufficient distance from it to see how it fits into the world as a whole. Instead, the fanatic takes his world to be primary and absolute. He does not see that his perspective is a version of something broader that escapes his full comprehension. He regards his own view of reality and his particular set of beliefs as the only genuine approaches to existence. This results in a fourth characteristic, which is that the fanatic will regard any men who fail to agree and conform to his view as possible threats or as outright opponents who must be controlled and perhaps defeated.

Although there may be only a few men who reveal these traits in all their extreme forms, there is little doubt that most of us exhibit some of these qualities at some time. Insofar as this is the case, freedom is in danger. A fanatical stance toward existence may arise partly because of the uncertainty and the open-ended character of life that freedom entails. The desire to hold fast to meanings that secure our existence is a pervasive factor in human life. However, it may be forgotten that human freedom and creativity play a part in all the meanings that we have and that our meanings are versions of the world and not exact copies of reality in itself. If these points are forgotten, meanings can come to be regarded as totally objective and absolute, and attempts may be made to impose them dogmatically on others. Then, instead of seeking meaning in an open-ended fashion, we may be forced to reduce human experience to fit patterns of meaning that are taken to be fixed and given.

At this time it ought to be pointed out that the narrowness of the fanatical character can infect some values or meanings only by distorting them or by changing them in important ways. An example of this fact involves the values of freedom and unity. A person may appear to be fanatical about trying to actualize a maximum degree of freedom and unity, but, if this happens, the ideas of freedom and unity must have a different character than they do in James's ethics. Freedom and unity are basic values which we combine into an existential norm to give us some guidance for decision-making in particular situations. However, this norm does not automatically prescribe specific actions. This suggests that the meaning of freedom and unity is not exhausted by a particular project or plan, or by a particular political structure or social order. Freedom and unity are open-ended values. As they stand in James's philosophy, they have a transcendent character. Their meaning cannot be narrowly fixed and tied to any single interpretation. To do this is to reduce the meaning of these values and to falsify them.

A person can be fanatical about a particular project or goal, but he cannot be fanatical about transcendent values such as freedom and unity. Freedom and unity are open-ended values, and the only genuine relationship that a man can have with them is one that searches openly for new ways to implement them. This relationship precludes the possibility of equating a particular course of action with the basic values themselves. However, this does not mean that our existential norm, which urges us to act so as to maximize freedom and unity, is purely formalistic and that it lacks concrete content. Our existential norm always functions in a particular set of circumstances. In those circumstances, it will help us to make a sound choice about the courses of action that will further man's well-being. Yet the particular course of action that is chosen may not be the only good one that is possible, and it will certainly not complete the implementation of freedom and unity. We will only be moving toward our goal. The open-ended character of freedom and unity and our existential norm will continue to lure us on, no matter what has happened already.

The fanatic may try to absolutize the relative in the case of freedom and unity. He may confuse a particular situation with freedom and unity themselves, but if these values are taken as they are, without reduction and distortion, they prohibit the possibility of a fanatical relationship to them. On the other hand, it is possible for a man to be devoted to values and norms with a transcendent character without distorting them by falling into fanaticism. This can be shown by describing the basic characteristics of the life of devotion. We can develop such a description by concentrating on the characteristics that would be the opposites of the four characteristics which stand at the center of the fanatical life.

First, although the devoted life is committed to projects and values which lead to concrete action in particular situations, this commitment is coupled with the understanding that one's dedication needs to be open so that it includes both a sensitivity to the interests of others and a self-conscious effort to escape dogmatism. The devoted man will not dismiss other points of view without investigating them openly and critically. He will not use reductive techniques of interpretation in order to preserve the primacy of his own position. This leads to a second feature of the genuine life of devotion. The devoted man will continue an active search for new evidence and data in the face of which his values and commitments can be tested. A questioning attitude will not be taken as a sign of weakening dedication or as a sign of a lost commitment. Rather, an attitude of questioning will be a way of keeping one's attention on the factors that are of essential importance and a way of clarifying those features as far as possible.

Thirdly, the devoted life is one that does not absolutize the relative. The devoted man recognizes that he lives in terms of a perspective that does not exhaust the world or human values, but that rather constitutes a version of them. The devoted man keeps some distance between his particular version of the world and the world as a whole. He sees that the latter is a broader horizon that may include a plurality of commitments. He tries to understand how all these components can fit together harmoniously, but he does not regard his own perspective as the only one that is authentic. These facts lead to a fourth characteristic. The devoted man's realization that his life constitutes a version of the world will make him sympathetic to the versions of other people. He is less likely to regard views that differ from his own as threats and as forms of opposition that must be controlled and defeated. He will recognize that the pervasive quality of freedom makes different interpretations possible and appropriate, and he will seek a positive value in the richness that this plurality affords. This does not preclude the possibility that the devoted man will desire to share his particular viewpoint with others and that he will even try to change the thinking of others, but he will do this without claiming infallibility for his own position.

At this point one other factor begins to emerge clearly. The devoted life points naturally toward values that have a transcendent quality. This life is open, and it seeks to understand the particularities of existence as components in a wide field or horizon. This understanding pushes one in the direction of a broad understanding of the pervasive and the universal structures of existence. In puzzling over the conditions that need to exist in order for there to be a desirable plurality of commitments and meanings in human life, the devoted man will be likely to find his attention focused on the values of freedom and unity. These values may, in fact, become the central motivating factors in the life of the devoted man. If this happens, his style of existence is well suited for such a relationship. The devoted man will see the importance of implementing freedom and unity in his concrete situations, but he will not confuse particular projects, goals, and institutions with freedom and unity themselves. He will see that the pursuit of the values of freedom and unity requires concrete action in present situations, but he will not absolutize the relative. The open-endedness of the values of freedom and unity will correspond with the openness in the life of the devoted man. At the same time the fact that freedom and unity are required for a meaningful existence creates an urgency for their implementation in human life that corresponds to the striving and the commitment to meaningful action that will characterize the life of devotion.

James believes that the quality of transcendence in the moral life can place ethics in a positive relation with religion. The values of freedom and unity are at the foundations of meaning, and through the appeal they make in our basic existential norm, these values lure us on toward an extension of meaning in human life. The man who is devoted to freedom and unity seeks to extend meaning. Although the devoted man does not have to be religious in order to be devoted, James does believe that faith in God fits with our concern for meaning, because it provides *promise* or *hope* that the basic values that we hold dear may have permanence. Freedom and unity also work in this direction. They extend a promise to man that meaning can be extended through human choices. This is implied in one of James's comments about the relation of pragmatism and some basic metaphysical concepts. Including the concepts of God and freedom in his account, James says, "Reducing, by the pragmatic test, the meaning of each of these concepts to its positive experienceable operation, I showed them all to mean the same thing, *viz.*, the presence of 'promise' in the world."[77]

The values of freedom and unity and a belief in God reveal a basis for human hope, and the religious life can reinforce moral concerns. One of the ways in which this reinforcement may take place involves our understanding of a basic characteristic of human life. Human existence is characterized by a restlessness. We exist in the present moment, but our awareness is not exhausted by our immediate situation. We are always on the move, looking ahead to something, seeking new things to do and new goals to test us. Man is a being who can see that his world and the quality of his personal life can be made better. He may also realize that this is best accomplished through the extension of freedom and unity. James's view of the relation between God and man suggests that in this awareness one's life may be touched by God.

James's understanding of the relation between God and man places a primary emphasis on man's responsibility to use his freedom to shape and to unify the details of his existence into meaningful and harmonious patterns. The existence of God also reveals an emphasis on freedom and unity. He can be viewed as seeking the maximum extension of these values in the world, and our use and extension of freedom and unity may contribute to his purposes. Thus, in the realization that we must extend freedom and unity for the sake of meaning, God may be luring us on. The sense of moral restlessness that we have may be a form of interaction with God. His relation to us can be felt in our restlessness, which pushes us forward continually and at the same time fills us with a hope that the process of existence and human striving do have an overarching meaning.

Whether the life of devotion is religiously oriented or not, the values of freedom and unity and the life of devotion are mutually supporting. The devoted man seeks meaning and value that will last for more than a moment. He seeks something that will unify his entire life. However, he sees that his own existence is only one version of the world and that his life fits into a broader horizon. Ultimately he may realize that this broader horizon involves the primary values of freedom and unity, which stand at the foundation of all choices involving commitments to ideals and to causes. This realization may culminate in a life that takes our existential norm as its basic principle for decision-making. On the other hand, the basic open-ended ideals of freedom and unity not only make the devoted life possible, but they call men to a devoted style of life. Freedom and unity require the kind of fruitful tension between commitment and openness that characterizes the devoted man. The devoted man will give himself to specific causes and projects that he thinks will further the implementation of human well-being. At the same time he will retain a sufficient distance between himself and these particular causes and goals so that he can alter his conduct to fit his critical understanding of the courses of action that are needed to move a changing world in a more fruitful direction.

The man who lives a life of devotion disciplines his own freedom. No man is forced to live this way, and the devoted life will not appear by chance. It constitutes a stance toward existence that is won and maintained only by great effort through time. If a man does not discipline his freedom in this way, however, distortion of human existence can occur. The transcendent goals will be replaced with something finite. The relative will be made absolute, and fanatical tendencies may set in with the harmful results that we noted earlier.

B. TOLERATION

The previous section of this chapter implies that the devoted man is tolerant of others. He has a genuine respect for the creative freedom of other men, and he is sensitive to the fact that there is positive value in life-styles that may differ from his own. However, some troublesome problems concerning toleration still need elaboration and clarification. They involve the nature of the position that the devoted man will take toward goals and interests that may conflict with his own. In other words, what are the proper limits of toleration?

Recalling some of the factors that make toleration important in James's philosophy will help us to suggest some answers to these problems. In society it is possible for the individual to make choices for various things, which attain some meaningful value for him simply because they are desired. Because of the possibility of conflict when choices are made, it is natural to seek compromises that allow for as much individual expression as possible. Since James is operating with the view that meaning is inextricably bound up with choice, toleration appears to be a helpful way of extending the factors of freedom and unity that allow for harmonious choosing and an increase of meaning. Here it is important to recall a point made in Chapter V. Toleration works in the service of freedom and unity, which are the primary values. Toleration frequently functions as an effective means of preserving and extending them, but the value of toleration is subordinate to the more basic values of freedom and unity.

If this order of priorities is not maintained, the concept of toleration can be developed and misused in ways that are detrimental to man's well-being. For example, in societies that restrict individual freedom in order to perpetuate the special interests of an elite ruling class or a dictator, a kind of toleration may be present. This will be a toleration that allows for a limited plurality of opinion so that the suppression of people is not so intense as to force violent revolution. By making minor concessions, those in power may keep their positions of authority, but the people under them will not experience the full range of freedom that is compatible with social harmony. A degree of genuine toleration may be present in such a society, but this toleration primarily serves the vested interests of a few and actually works against the maximum extension of freedom that would fit with a harmonious communal life.

There is another way in which toleration becomes an ambiguous value when it is divorced from our understanding of freedom and unity. This revolves around the implications of making toleration absolute both in its extension and in its pri-

macy as a moral value. Such a consistent absolutizing of toleration by an individual or a group means that the individual or
the group must tolerate everything. A total permissiveness will
reign. This attitude may create a situation that is ripe for ruth-
less uses of power by other men that will result in the eventual
suppression of freedom. Such actions might be criticized by
those who advocate absolute toleration, but the actions could
not strictly speaking be stopped by persons who consistently
absolutized toleration.

As James suggests, the purpose of toleration is to allow
people to pursue their interests without interference, so long as
those interests do not jeopardize the greatest possible extension
of harmonious uses of freedom in the community. This means
that some acts and choices may have restrictions placed upon
them. The decisions that establish the boundaries of toleration
will, of course, need to be largely dependent on the facts of the
particular situations involved and on the clarity with which the
people involved can see the ramifications of the possible
choices. Risk and ambiguity cannot be eliminated, but the basic
question that will focus the thinking of those who are responsible for establishing priorities will be: What acts will tend to
maximize freedom and unity in this situation? Courses of action
that maximize freedom and unity will be given priority, and
the boundaries of toleration will be determined accordingly.

This means that the extension of toleration may vary from
time to time. For example, in some instances of national crisis
or communal life, the protection and extension of freedom and
unity will require a more restricted understanding of toleration
than will be the case in other circumstances. Of course, everyone may not agree about the nature of the restrictions and the
situations in which restrictions will need to be imposed. If
there is disagreement, the first course of action should be to
engage in analysis, discussion, and debate to see how grievances can be settled.

To work well, this approach requires good faith among the
parties involved and an openness to others. These qualities
may be difficult to achieve and guarantee. This means that the

value of processes of debate and discussion can be morally ambiguous. It is well known that so-called rational debate can be used to support vested interests that produce injustice and discrimination. Moreover, it is not always easy to tell when a discussion or debate is being held in good faith and when it is taking place in bad faith. Nevertheless, debate and discussion are courses of action that must be urged and pursued with great vigor wherever there is a need to settle disagreements. Even though the value of these methods may not be free of ambiguity, it is likely to be less ambiguous than other alternatives for the settlement of differences.

Alternatives involving disruption and violence, for example, may in fact lead to a better community over the long run, but they do so only with great waste and expense. In addition to the sheer physical destruction that may occur, these courses of action are never free from the creation of intense feelings of mistrust, hatred, and revenge. These factors are all detrimental to the existence of unity and cooperation, and without these freedom is crippled. Discussion and debate can lead to just solutions of problems without these negative factors. In fact, the process of debate and discussion can be the occasion for the building up of trust, friendship, and cooperation. These reasons are sufficient for giving priority to the processes of open debate and discussion wherever grievances exist.

On the other hand, even though courses of action that utilize the methods of disruption and violence are never unequivocally good, they may be the lesser of evils in some situations, and, therefore, they cannot be totally ruled out as courses of action that are morally justified. In general, justification of such courses of action will be forthcoming only when a critical and an open analysis of a situation reveals that a proper balance between freedom and unity is being destroyed and when there appears to be no hope of reversing the trend by other means that are less destructive. There is no absolute criterion in human existence to determine when such points of crisis are reached. Here human finitude leaves us with fundamental moral ambiguity. However, we can say that before any decision to act violently is morally justified, men must have pursued nonviolent courses of action in good faith and with vigor. Further, they must have thought critically about the facts and the consequences of their actions, and their decision to act violently must be grounded in devotion to the basic values of freedom and unity.

In the actual world, the devoted man is not likely to be infinitely tolerant in every situation. He will have to sift out ideas and claims very carefully in order to decide which ones genuinely support and extend human well-being. He will give an open hearing to various plans of action, but this does not mean that he will need to allow all courses of action. His understanding of toleration will be that it is a moving and a flexible dimension of freedom which may need to be restricted in some situations. On the other hand, the devoted man will seek to extend toleration wherever possible because it is one of the concrete meanings of freedom. Perhaps the conditions under which toleration can be taken as absolute will never exist, but the work of the devoted man will seek to establish these conditions as far as possible.

Whenever he can the devoted man will pursue his goals in a manner that is open and nonviolent. He may ultimately have to use violence, although more positive measures will always be given priority because of the vast destruction that violence involves. In reaching his decisions about what to do, the man who exemplifies the highest traits of the devoted life will emphasize the following: (1) What are the facts of the matter? (2) What are the particular courses of action that imaginative thinking presents, and what are their consequences likely to be? (3) Which course of action seems the most likely to maximize freedom and unity? He will then act on the plan that best seems to do the latter. Moral reflection about all these factors requires openness and a basic honesty. There is no way to assure these qualities in decision-making except through communal and personal training and discipline, but the life of the devoted man is disciplined in this way, and it will reveal these qualities to a high degree.

C. A Concluding Comment

Existence is always particular and specific, but it is also shot full of vagueness and ambiguity. The devoted man recognizes this as he strives for moral clarity. He may also see that philosophy is one attempt to cope with the ambiguity in human life. Its analyses give us some insights about the general factors that we must take into account in order to make good ethical decisions. However, this analysis does not by itself tell us specifically what to do. That insight can be obtained only by plunging ourselves into the particular facts and situations where all our decisions are finally grounded. James's entire philosophy and his moral views in particular reflect this movement between the general and the particular. At the same time his perspective calls our attention to the ambiguity in existence. This ambiguity cannot be entirely eliminated from our lives, but it may be understood to some degree. Ambiguity is grounded in structures that can be grasped. This theme permeates James's thought, and it leads to some interesting conclusions about the moral life which we will draw out in the next chapter.

IX

Freedom and Ambiguity

N O PHILOSOPHER SAYS as much as he should. The richness and vastness of existence escape full comprehension and ultimately reduce him to silence. With more time and greater energy he might be able to say more, but time and energy are limited and thought ceases. Nevertheless, a good philosopher will give us some clarity about our existence, and at the same time his thought will be sufficiently rich to point us toward important ideas and problems that are implicit in his thought but never brought to light fully. These problems and ideas can become the subject matter for future thinkers. They may take these problems and ideas and bring them into sharper focus. This analysis fits the philosophy of William James. We have already seen that his philosophy contains implications for ethics which can be elaborated and unified into a moral theory that is both consistent with his explicit statements and extended beyond them. These developments show how we can develop a moral norm that will help us to make good choices in an existence that is so full of possibility that it is ambiguous.

Ambiguity is one of the topics to which James invites our attention, and the concept is important in interpreting his philosophy. James helps us to see what it means to live in a world that is ambiguous, but he does not say all that he could about the ramifications of this ambiguity for the moral life. This chapter will draw out James's philosophy in this area. In particular, we will focus our attention on one manifestation of ambiguity in the moral life. This manifestation involves disagreements that men may have on moral issues. It raises questions such as the following: (1) Can men employ basic ethical principles, such as our existential norm, using them with honesty, openness, and a critical understanding of facts and consequences of proposed courses of action, and still make different decisions when faced by the problem? (2) If so, what does this say about the structure of the moral life and the tasks of philosophical ethics?

A. Ambiguity and Meaning

We can answer the questions posed above only if we can be clear about the nature of ambiguity. Ambiguity is most commonly regarded as a quality of some ideas or beliefs. When an idea or a belief is unclear, paradoxical, or susceptible to a variety of interpretations, we can say that it is ambiguous. If we start with this notion of ambiguity, there are at least two interpretations that can follow. One is the result of a rationalistic approach. It would say that ambiguity is only a property of ideas or beliefs, and that existence, or reality as a whole, is not ambiguous. Rather, reality as a whole has a fixed structure and meaning that are in principle perfectly clear and intelligible. Man's task in this world is to use his reason correctly so that he grasps this structure and meaning and eliminates ambiguity from the sphere of ideas and beliefs.

This view has implications for moral theory. One of the most important is that there is always a single action that is morally the best in a particular situation. If there is no ambiguity in existence, there will be only one genuine standard of value. Moreover, this standard will be structured so that only one action in a situation can be the moral ideal. Again, man's basic problem is to discover the genuine standard of value and the particular actions that it decrees. This means that the creative role of freedom is radically curtailed. Freedom is understood primarily as a capacity to conform to the established meanings discovered by reason or to rebel against them. Freedom does not properly have a function to create and to establish value and clarity, since the true values and the genuine clarity of things are already fixed.

James's philosophy is a reaction against this way of thinking. He moves toward a second line of thought that does not simply make ambiguity the product of a human intellect that is weak or improperly used. James does not deny that the human mind has limitations and that much ambiguity does enter human life because man's reason is used uncritically. In fact, his recognition of these points leads directly to his development of pragmatism. It is a way to overcome ambiguity by finding an empirical process for making our ideas clear and for ascertaining their truth. Nevertheless, this same pragmatism also implies that ambiguity is not merely a quality of some of our ideas and beliefs. Instead, James's theory implies that the category of ambiguity may require a place of prominence in any adequate account of being as a whole. James himself believes that pragmatism ultimately points toward a world that is pluralistic in character. This is a world of freedom. It is a world that is full of possibilities and novel outcomes. This means that as we look toward the future from the present, the outcome of the future is uncertain. It is not merely the case that our ideas or our beliefs are unclear with respect to what will be, but, rather, reality as a whole is always moving ambiguously to some degree.

Our world is in process. Sameness and identity are only relative qualities. Present circumstances contain possibilities for the future that are vast, and we have to rest content with probabilities in our judgments. In the world that James describes, ambiguity is even a category for God. James's view suggests that God may see all of the possibilities that any present state of affairs points to, and in this respect his knowledge may be complete. But if there is freedom in the radical sense that James has in mind, God's knowledge about what will be actual is always growing but also incomplete. The effect will be that as God looks toward the future from his present perspective, he will also see that a present set of circumstances can point in a number of different directions, but which one in particular will occur is not certain. Ambiguity exists wherever there are multiple possibilities for meaning and existence. The rationalistic position is correct in saying that ambiguity may be found in ideas and beliefs. But this position does not go far enough for James because it fails to see that ambiguity is a pervasive character of reality as a whole.

Man is a being who consciously seeks to give himself identity by bringing particular patterns of meaning to light in this pluralistic and ambiguous world. The fact that existence is ambiguous can be both a positive and a negative factor in our quest to find identity and meaning. Ambiguity can be a positive factor because it means both that numerous options are open for human choice and that choice is an essential factor in the actualization of possible states of affairs. Meaning requires the feeling that a man is actually accomplishing something novel through his choices and that his striving is making a difference to the future outcome of existence. The fact that through his choices a man can move his world and his existence from a position of ambiguity to one of relative clarity indicates that new patterns of meaning are being brought to light and that man's striving is making a difference to the future outcomes of the world's process.

A man's life actualizes one possible way of existence no matter how it is lived. Moreover, his life will always be influencing future outcomes. However, the quest for meaning that men engage in moves them to try to achieve a sense of personal identity that implies continuity and order in the self. If ambiguity in the world is a positive factor in providing a plurality of opportunities, it is also a potential negative factor in the attempt to achieve the continuity of meaning that goes with a full sense of identity. Faced by a wide plurality of possibilities and options for meaning, a person may be unsuccessful in shaping an overarching meaning for his life which he can maintain through time and which will also serve to sustain him in times of difficulty. For example, he may begin to cultivate one course of action only to be distracted by another. Once oriented in a new direction, he may find it difficult to accept what he has been, and he will lose continuity with his past. If such a process continues, as it does in some lives, unity and overall direction will never appear. Instead, there will be fragmentation and perhaps a sense of the loss of meaning. Existence may take on the quality of absurdity.

The interesting thing to note, however, is that feelings of meaninglessness and absurdity may not always be due to a lack of possibilities. Instead they may be due to the fact that there is too much possibility for meaning. Human existence may be so full of potential that it is baffling to some individuals, and thus it comes to strike them as lacking meaning. Every man is given the chance to find himself, but no man is assured success in this pursuit. In order for every man to have his chance, the possibilities are vast, but their wide scope may prove too much for some.

Some philosophers who focus on the reality of ambiguity and the human quest for meaning fail to take full account of the richness of possibility that is implied by ambiguity. A philosopher such as Sartre, for example, wants to focus our attention on the vast range of possibilities in human life, and he urges us toward honest choice of a course of action that makes sense to us. However, in laying out his view of existence it becomes clear that religious commitments are suspect. They are ways of dodging the freedom and the ambiguity of existence by orienting one's life in terms of an absolute power who determines the priorities of meaning and value for us. James wants to rule out theological determinism just as Sartre does, but James is more open and subtle than Sartre in analyzing the meaning of ambiguity in existence.

The very fact that existence is ambiguous leads James to support the authenticity of some religious commitments. Some religious commitments are attempts to flee from freedom and shared evidence about our world, but not all of them are this way. In an ambiguous world it is not only possible to have a variety of views about God, some of which will be compatible with the best empirical evidence and which will also allow for a radical sense of human freedom, but there is also room for the hope that meaning may extend beyond the human sphere and find its fulfillment in that which is Transcendent. If the possibility of hope is not ruled out dogmatically, some men will want to stretch themselves toward the future in such a way that they will seek something beyond finitude and death. Ambiguity leaves us with an uncertainty and a risk in our commitments, but it also makes room for faith and for religious commitments that are authentic. The potential of existence may be baffling, but the possibilities for hope that this richness affords ought not to be restricted unnecessarily.

B. Ambiguity and the Moral Life

Ambiguity also affects the moral life. Moral reflection is one of the ways that men use to order their lives into meaningful patterns. It involves disciplined analysis about what one ought to do and about the implementation of ideals in a community. Again, James's emphasis on the prominence of ambiguity in existence implies that he takes a position different from that of the rationalist in trying to understand the structure of the moral life. The rationalist looks at moral problems with the idea that proper thinking ought to culminate in a single decision that is absolutely the best course of action. All other possible courses of action are more or less in error. Ethical reflection ought to produce universal agreement, and insofar as it does not, we are either failing to use the right principles and orderings of value, or we are applying these standards incorrectly, or our intellect is clouded in some other respect.

James's philosophy opposes these ideas, although it does not go so far as some contemporary reactions against rationalism, which reduce ethical judgments to expressions of emotion and which largely remove ethical judgments and disagreements from the sphere of rational discourse. James believes that morality is dependent on a careful use of man's capacities for thought, but his view about the structure of the world and these capacities differs from that of the rationalist. In James's view, a man is a part of a world that is in process and that is only partly ordered in terms of values. Not only is this world capable of development, but its meaning and its values are inextricably related to human freedom and creativity. Man has the task of shaping his own world. This task extends to the development of ethical guidelines that help us to solve conflicts and enable us to make good decisions that extend man's possibilities for meaning.

Ambiguity appears all along the way as we try to make good decisions. The complexity of the facts is one factor here. Although we sometimes say that the facts speak for themselves, it is often the case that they do not speak clearly. The facts have to be interpreted, evaluated, and weighed, and we have already seen that there may be a plurality of interpretations that fit and perhaps that fit well. The meaning of the facts is not a fixed property in them, but it is something that is drawn out and developed over time, and more than one meaning may be extracted. In addition, when we propose courses of action for the future there are more ambiguities concerning the possible outcomes and the consequences. Human finitude forces ambiguity on us at this point, but even if all the possibilities were known, there would still be uncertainty about the particular ones that will become actual. The best information we can ever get on such questions is a degree of probability based on fallible calculations.

A lack of clarity is not always due to a clouded intellect, and even if we are operating with an ethical norm such as the one we have proposed, ambiguity can still be present. In fact, people may apply a basic ethical principle to the same problem with openness, honesty, and as much knowledge of the facts and consequences of proposed courses of action as it is possible to get and still emerge with different interpretations and decisions about the most desirable ways to proceed. What are we to say from James's perspective if this happens?

In the case of our existential norm, we might decide that it is inadequate because it may fail to give us total agreement on a single course of action even when we are thinking openly and critically. However, in James's analysis, such an approach is too rationalistic. In a world of freedom, it is possible and even likely that there will be a plurality of interpretations and decisions that fit with the facts and an application of the norm. This is because the facts are not static and fixed with respect to their meaning and with respect to the outcomes that are really possible. If the norm we are using rules out no courses of action, it is not of any use. But if it rules out some courses of action and leaves some standing, that may be as much as we can expect. Thus, one of the important conclusions that follows from James's position is that we may face a moral problem in a present situation and find that more than one course of action is morally justifiable.

Although sound moral decisions are not indefinitely numerous in a situation, they may be multiple. This suggests that some of our disagreements about moral problems may ultimately rest on a needless rigidity and dogmatism in claiming that there is only one acceptable course of action. We tend to operate with the view that there always must be one single interpretation or alternative that is the best, but this view may be mistaken. In present situations there may be a plurality of interpretations and courses of action open to us that will lead to a speedy and equitable extension of human well-being. The realization of this fact may in itself lead to a greater degree of cooperation and openness among men.

The awareness that more than one action may be morally justified in a particular set of circumstances can help us to understand another feature of the moral life. The nature of existence is such that an individual will have to stand by some interpretation of existence, and he will have to decide to act in particular ways. As he works out his interpretation and makes his decisions, he may make an appeal to what has traditionally been called *conscience*. This concept is easily misused. Conscience is sometimes regarded as a source of infallible moral directives. Moreover, appeals to conscience are often employed to give a stamp of approval to uncritical intuitions and acts of unwarranted destruction and selfishness. In spite of these facts, the concept still points to a basic positive feature of the moral life. In its highest sense, an appeal to conscience as a basis for action means that we are acting in accord with the most critical and sensitive moral reflection that we can perform. The concept is properly used when it refers to careful deliberation based on sound moral principles and carried out with openness, honesty, knowledge of facts, and the attempt to calculate the consequences of future actions.

At the same time, conscience is also an important moral category because it implies that there may be moral disagreements after such reflection has taken place. Appeals to conscience are usually made in situations where one senses that there will be a difference of opinion. Unless a person takes a dogmatic and fanatical position with respect to his own conscience, he will recognize that other men may reflect critically and reach a decision different from his own. Thus, the highest appeal to conscience is a way of saying that *in a specific situation, critical analysis, so far as I have been able to carry it out, leads me to act in a particular direction. I am true to myself in the action that I take, but I also recognize my limitations and my fallibility.* The man who acts in terms of our existential norm concerning freedom and unity will be likely to make such appeals to conscience, for he recognizes that he lives in a world of uncertainties and ambiguities. He realizes that he must make particular choices. However, he chooses with the awareness that a plurality of courses of action may work beneficially for the human community and with the understanding that there is no final assurance that his course of action is absolutely the best.

These suggestions will influence our attempts to evaluate ourselves and other people from a moral point of view. When we judge the moral worth of any person, we will always be interested in the consequences of his actions. At the same time, we will be interested in the process of thought that leads to a course of action and a set of consequences. Good moral consequences may sometimes occur in spite of a lack of critical and sensitive moral reflection, and bad consequences may sometimes occur in spite of the presence of this kind of thought. However, neither situation is likely to be the case very often. Usually, good consequences follow from sound reflection, and bad consequences follow from a lack of it. Critical and sensitive reflection is at the heart of the moral life, and the way that a person thinks will be one of the chief tests for judging his moral worth.

It will be important to ask the following questions in this regard. Is a person sensitive to the human need for meaning? Is he sensitive to the importance of freedom and unity as the conditions for extending meaning? Does he seek for a wide grasp of facts, and does he attempt to achieve clarity about the possible results of proposed courses of action? If we can give positive answers to these questions as we try to understand a human being, and if these positive qualities are coupled with the courage to act in order to extend freedom and unity, we will be dealing with a highly developed moral life. The particular decisions that such a man will make in specific situations must await a careful contextual analysis, but he will approach all situations with a general framework that will help to bring order and human well-being out of dilemmas and problems.

C. CONCLUSION

The presence of ambiguity in human existence leads to an ethical perspective that is both principle-oriented and situational in its analyses. We seek general guidelines to help us order the ambiguity, but to get sound decisions we always have to plunge back into the particular circumstances in which we live. Human situations, however, always point in a variety of directions, and ambiguity is never completely eliminated. We are even left with the possibility of disagreement after careful moral analysis. For some men this possibility of disagreement may seem like the repudiation of all genuine morality. It may seem to them to open the doors to every kind of excess and to the moral justification of any act performed.

Yet these conclusions will not follow if we remember that there is a basic norm at work in the analysis of the moral life that we have presented. Moreover, we are fully able to use the experience of the past. This experience can be cast in the forms of rules and precedents. Although we will not want to be bound to these guidelines absolutely, we can consult them in making our decisions and in judging those of others. If all these factors are applied with honesty and openness, which, of course, no one can guarantee, some courses of action will be ruled out as narrow, self-centered, and destructive of freedom and unity. However, there may still be a number of options left, and individuals must choose the ones that they find the most adequate.

The emphasis that we have placed on openness, honesty, critical reflection about facts and consequences, and the need to obtain general guidelines for decision-making indicates that it is a difficult task to live a moral life. The moral life is a way of existing that one learns as he lives, and a person is never more than on the way toward becoming moral so long as his life goes on. A person gets his start at the hands of others. Parents, teachers, and friends can instill in a young person an appreciation of honesty and openness. They can help him to experience the meaning that comes from a creative use of his powers for choice and action. They can also put him on the way toward learning how to think critically, how to be sensitive to evidence, and how to appreciate the value of freedom, discipline, and harmony. The person who lacks these benefits while he is young will find it harder to live a moral existence, but it can be done. On the other hand, good training is no assurance of success, and the person who has received good training in the areas noted will have to continue to develop the benefits he has received if he is to move along on his way toward the moral life.

Freedom is at the heart of the human self, and since freedom produces ambiguity, there is ambiguity in the self. This ambiguity manifests itself in the fact that a man learns who he is only as he chooses and acts, and yet as long as he lives his tasks of choosing and acting are never complete. Man's freedom always places him on the way somewhere, but just where is never totally clear. Clarity begins to emerge only as freedom disciplines itself and tries to achieve a consistent meaning through time. The attitude toward existence that we have drawn out of James's moral philosophy provides a goal that can help to give one a sense of clarity about who he is, where he is situated, and where he is going.

This attitude stresses a pursuit of meaning through the extension of the values of freedom and unity, which are the basic conditions for full human existence. This style of life unifies the self by urging one to serve men through the extension of the prerequisites for meaningful existence. The demands of this moral life are great. There is no assurance that a person will be able to meet every requirement it brings forth, but the reward for trying is an ordered existence and a sense of meaning that will not cease to grow.

The situation left to us by our analysis of ambiguity and the moral life fits James's philosophy as a whole. Uncertainty, risk, and hope are combined. Rationalistic absolutes have been eliminated in his description of man's predicament, and the result is the appearance of a greater degree of ambiguity in existence than we may have sensed originally. These factors point toward uncertainty and risk, but there is also the hope that through a disciplined use of freedom, men will not be swallowed up by uncertainty or terrified by risk. Instead, they will strive with courage in the midst of ambiguity, and they will bring new extensions of freedom, unity, and meaning to human life.

A Chronology of William James's Life

1842	Born in New York City on January 11
1860–1861	Studies painting with William M. Hunt at Newport, Rhode Island
1863–1864	Begins his studies at the Harvard School of Medicine
1865–1866	Accompanies Louis Agassiz on a scientific expedition to Brazil
1869	Receives his M.D. degree from the Harvard School of Medicine
1872	Becomes an Instructor of Physiology at Harvard
1875	Teaches his first course in psychology
1876	Becomes Assistant Professor of Physiology at Harvard
1878	Marries Alice Howe Gibbens on July 10, and signs a contract with Henry Holt and Company to write a text on psychology
1879	Teaches his first course in philosophy
1880	Becomes Assistant Professor of Philosophy at Harvard
1885	Becomes Professor of Philosophy at Harvard
1889	Becomes Professor of Psychology at Harvard
1890	Publication of *The Principles of Psychology*
1897	Publication of *The Will to Believe, and Other Essays in Popular Philosophy*
1898	Lectures on pragmatism in California
1901–1902	Gives the Gifford Lectures at the University of Edinburgh
1902	Publication of his Gifford Lectures under the title *The Varieties of Religious Experience*
1906	Visiting Professor at Stanford University
1906–1907	Gives lectures on pragmatism at the Lowell Institute in Boston and at Columbia University

1907   Publication of *Pragmatism* and resignation from Harvard

1908   Gives the Hibbert Lectures at Oxford

1909   Publication of his Hibbert Lectures under the title *A Pluralistic Universe*

1910   Dies on August 26, at his summer home in Chocorua, New Hampshire

Notes

1. For an excellent biography of James which helps to bring out these points, see Gay Wilson Allen, *William James* (The Viking Press, 1967).

2. Two authors have devoted considerable time to James's ethics. See two books by Ralph Barton Perry, *In the Spirit of William James* (Indiana University Press, 1958) and *The Thought and Character of William James*, 2 vols. (Little, Brown and Company, 1935). See also a more recent work by Bernard P. Brennan, *The Ethics of William James* (College and University Press Services, Inc., 1962). One strength of these accounts is that they stress James's pervasive interest in ethical problems. On the other hand, the work of Perry and Brennan also has certain gaps. Perry's accounts are largely biographical, and they leave basic questions unanswered concerning the foundations and the adequacy of James's ethics. While Brennan's treatment does more on these points, it underplays the role of the value of freedom in James's ethics and does not adequately interpret the situational approach to decision-making that James advocates.

3. The following literature is pertinent to this point: Julius Seelye Bixler, "The Existentialists and William James," *The American Scholar*, Vol. XXVIII, No. 1 (Winter, 1958–1959), pp. 80–90; Geoffrey Clive, *The Romantic Enlightenment* (Meridian Books, The World Publishing Company, 1960); James M. Edie, "Notes on the Philosophical Anthropology of William James," *An Invitation to Phenomenology*, ed. by James M. Edie (Quadrangle Books, Inc., 1965), pp. 110–132; John Wild, *Existence and the World of Freedom* (Prentice-Hall, Inc., 1963); John Wild, "William James and

Existential Authenticity," *The Journal of Existentialism*, Vol. V, No. 19 (Spring, 1965), pp. 243–256.

4. In conjunction with the idea that consciousness is intentional and selective, it is worth noting that James's theory of consciousness was a positive influence on the thinking of Edmund Husserl, whose phenomenological approach to philosophy in general and theory of the intentionality of consciousness in particular had an important impact on the work of Heidegger, Sartre, and Merleau-Ponty. For discussions of the relations between James's theory of consciousness and Husserl's phenomenology, see Edie, *op. cit.*; Aron Gurwitsch, *The Field of Consciousness* (Duquesne University Press, 1964); Johannes Linschoten, *Auf dem Wege zu einer Phä-nomenologischen Psychologie: Die Psychologie von William James*, tr. from the Dutch by Frank Monk (Berlin: Walter de Gruyter and Company, 1961); Alfred Schutz, "William James' Concept of the Stream of Thought Phenomenologically Interpreted," *Philosophy and Phenomenological Research*, Vol. I, No. 4 (June, 1941), pp. 442–452; Herbert Spiegelberg, *The Phenomenological Movement*, 2 vols. (The Hague: Martinus Nijhoff, 1960). The latter work is especially significant in this regard.

5. Dewey's writings are of special importance here. In particular, see John Dewey and James H. Tufts, *Ethics* (Henry Holt & Co., Inc., 1908) and John Dewey, *Human Nature and Conduct* (Modern Library, Inc., 1930).

6. For examples of recent literature relevant to this point, see Joseph Fletcher, *Situation Ethics: The New Morality* (The Westminster Press, 1966), and *Moral Responsibility: Situation Ethics at Work* (The Westminster Press, 1967). Also relevant is *The Situation Ethics Debate*, ed. by Harvey Cox (The Westminster Press, 1968).

7. William James, *The Principles of Psychology* (Dover Publications, Inc., 1950), Vol. I, p. 1. Hereafter referred to as *Principles*.

8. For example, see *Principles*, Vol. I, p. 185.

9. See *ibid.*, Vol. I, pp. 196 ff. Although James does not develop an elaborate phenomenological method such as that worked out by Husserl, the notion of the "psychologist's fallacy" is similar to Husserl's idea of the *epoché* or the process of "bracketing." The Husserlian idea emphasizes the need for the investigator to try to suspend his present attitudes and beliefs in order to allow the phenomena under examination to appear in a light that is as un-biased as possible. In understanding human experience the purpose

of this "bracketing" is to enable the investigator to grasp experiences as they are actually being lived through. James's efforts in guarding against the "psychologist's fallacy" are clearly in line with this goal. Both Husserl and James want a clear understanding of human experiences so that they can clarify and describe what is central and universal in the life of consciousness.

10. *Principles,* Vol. I, p. 197.

11. These themes are present at many points in James's writings. Examples include the following: *Principles,* Vol. I, p. 139; "Reflex Action and Theism," *The Will to Believe, and Other Essays in Popular Philosophy* (Dover Publications, Inc., 1956), p. 117; "The Sentiment of Rationality," *The Will to Believe, and Other Essays in Popular Philosophy,* p. 77. "Reflex Action and Theism" appeared originally in the *Unitarian Review* for October, 1881. "The Sentiment of Rationality" appeared in various versions between 1879 and 1882.

With respect to the idea that consciousness is stretched out in time, James points out that present experience is surrounded and shaped by the effects and meanings of past experiences and future possibilities. While making this point in *The Principles of Psychology,* James develops his doctrine of "fringes." (See Vol. I, pp. 258 ff.) Human experience consists primarily of a present focal point that is "fringed" by a wide variety of contents (spatial, temporal, perceptual, conceptual, etc.). This "fringe" provides the background against which the primary object of attention is focused. The "fringe" features of a conscious state are not at the center of attention, but they do much to give the center of attention its particular quality. In addition, "fringe" contents may move into the center of attention if the focus of attention is altered. This view of "fringes" was one of the ideas that most attracted Husserl when he read *The Principles of Psychology,* and in one form or another the concept continues to play an important part in contemporary phenomenology and existential thought.

12. See *Principles,* Vol. I, p. 140.

13. *Ibid.,* Vol. I, pp. 284–285.

14. *Ibid.,* Vol. I, p. 286.

15. See William James, "Great Men and Their Environment," *The Will to Believe, and Other Essays in Popular Philosophy,* p. 219. The essay was originally published in the *Atlantic Monthly* for October, 1880.

16. See *Principles,* Vol. I, pp. 133 ff.

17. *Ibid.*, Vol. I, p. 141.

18. *Ibid.*, Vol. I, p. 224. James's attack on the attempts to analyze experience in terms of atomistic sense impressions anticipates some of the insights stressed in recent phenomenology. For example, see Maurice Merleau-Ponty, *The Phenomenology of Perception*, tr. by Colin Smith (Humanities Press, Inc., 1962), pp. 3–63.

19. *Principles*, Vol. I, p. 339.

20. *Ibid.*, Vol. I, p. 241. The emphasis that James places on bodily feeling and on the difference that it makes for consciousness to be embodied is also found in his *Essays in Radical Empiricism* (Longmans, Green, & Co., 1958), pp. 65 ff., 150–154, and 168–171. Again James's comments anticipate recent developments. Examples include his ideas about the perpetual presence of bodily feeling and the effect of embodiment on our perception of space. These suggestions can also be fruitfully compared with Merleau-Ponty's *The Phenomenology of Perception*, especially pp. 67–153. James's contributions in illuminating the role of the body in self-hood and prereflexive experience are also stressed in Johannes Linschoten's *Auf dem Wege zu einer Phänomenologischen Psychologie: Die Psychologie von William James.*

21. *Principles*, Vol. I, p. 293.

22. *Ibid.*, Vol. I, p. 297.

23. James claims that we actually feel this part of the self and that the feelings are bodily in character. The body is present at this level of selfhood, although our attention is directed more specifically to particular functions of the conscious body at this stage of analysis.

24. See *Principles*, Vol. I, p. 315.

25. *Principles*, Vol. II, p. 571.

26. See *Ibid.*, p. 572.

27. Although it is clear that James is talking about freedom, he prefers to use the term "chance" in this essay, because he believes that the meaning of "freedom" has been distorted by some determinists. Some of these philosophers use the concept of freedom when speaking about human actions that are performed without constraint from forces external to oneself. Of course, even these actions are in the end regarded as determined totally by factors in one's past. James thinks this is a bogus use of the term "freedom." Thus, in this context he uses a different term to avoid confusion and to convey the sense of freedom that he has in mind. See "The Dilemma of Determinism," *The Will to Believe, and Other Essays*

in *Popular Philosophy,* pp. 148 ff. The essay first appeared in the *Unitarian Review* for September, 1884.

28. See William James, "The Sentiment of Rationality," *The Will to Believe, and Other Essays in Popular Philosophy,* pp. 63–110.

29. William James, *The Letters of William James,* ed. by his son Henry James (Atlantic Monthly Press, 1920), Vol. I, p. 147.

30. See "The Dilemma of Determinism," *The Will to Believe, and Other Essays in Popular Philosophy,* p. 146; *Principles,* Vol. II, pp. 573 ff.

31. *Principles,* Vol. II, p. 573.

32. *Ibid.,* Vol. I, p. 218.

33. See *ibid.,* Vol. I, p. 221; William James, "The Function of Cognition," *Pragmatism* (Meridian Books, The World Publishing Company, 1963), pp. 209 ff. "The Function of Cognition" was read before the Aristotelian Society in December, 1884, and it was published in *Mind* in the following year. James made the distinction between "knowledge of acquaintance" and "knowledge-about" early in his career, and he retained it throughout his life. In particular, it is at the center of the distinctions between perception and conception that play a part in his pragmatism.

34. *Principles,* Vol. II, p. 661.

35. See "The Sentiment of Rationality," *The Will to Believe, and Other Essays in Popular Philosophy,* p. 92.

36. *Ibid.,* p. 110.

37. Quoted from Perry, *The Thought and Character of William James,* Vol. II, p. 263.

38. Quoted from *ibid.,* Vol. II, p. 264. Although it is beyond the scope of this book, the influence of Josiah Royce (1855–1916) on James's ethical position is worth noting. Royce was James's friend and colleague at Harvard, and James's ideas in "The Moral Philosopher and the Moral Life" were partly shaped by his study of Royce's book, *The Religious Aspect of Philosophy,* which was published in 1885. In that work Royce made use of his "moral insight" in developing an idealistic metaphysics. Although James disagreed strongly with the conclusions of Royce's idealism, James saw that basic features of Royce's ethical analysis could also be used in other philosophical perspectives.

39. Quoted from Perry, *The Thought and Character of William James,* Vol. II, p. 265.

40. William James, "The Moral Philosopher and the Moral Life," *The Will to Believe, and Other Essays in Popular Philosophy,*

p. 184. The essay first appeared in the *International Journal of Ethics* in April, 1891.

41. See *ibid.*, p. 184.

42. *Ibid.*, pp. 184–185.

43. See *ibid.*, p. 185.

44. See *ibid.*, p. 189.

45. *Ibid.*, p. 190.

46. *Ibid.*, p. 193.

47. *Ibid.*, p. 194.

48. *Ibid.*, p. 197.

49. See *ibid.*, p. 201. The term "demand" should be taken as synonymous with "choice" or "claim" which frees it from a flavor of dogmatism and militancy to some degree. No doubt some choices will be made militantly and dogmatically, but this is certainly not a condition that must be present in order for them to be considered.

50. See *ibid.*, p. 203.

51. *Ibid.*, p. 205.

52. *Ibid.*

53. See *ibid.*, p. 209.

54. *Ibid.*, p. 206.

55. See *ibid.*, p. 209.

56. *The Will to Believe, and Other Essays in Popular Philosophy*, p. x.

57. "The Will to Believe," *The Will to Believe, and Other Essays in Popular Philosophy*, p. 3.

58. *Ibid.*, p. 30.

59. William James, "On a Certain Blindness in Human Beings," *Talks to Teachers on Psychology: and to Students on Some of Life's Ideals* (W. W. Norton & Company, Inc., 1958), p. 150.

60. *Ibid.*, p. 169.

61. See William James, *The Varieties of Religious Experience* (Random House, Inc., 1955), p. 232. All references are to the Modern Library edition.

62. See *ibid.*, pp. 16 ff.

63. *Ibid.*, p. 333.

64. See *ibid.*, pp. 266–267.

65. *Ibid.*, pp. 354–355.

66. *Ibid.*, p. 356.

67. See *ibid.*, p. 348.

68. *Ibid.*, p. 366.

69. See *ibid.*, p. 368.

70. William James, *A Pluralistic Universe* (Longmans, Green, & Co., 1909), p. 311.

71. Charles S. Peirce, *Collected Papers*, ed. by Charles Hartshorne and Paul Weiss (Harvard University Press, 1931–1935), Vol. V, p. 402.

72. William James, *Pragmatism* (Meridian Books, The World Publishing Company, 1963), p. 133.

73. *Ibid.*, p. 133.

74. *Ibid.*, p. 145.

75. The idea of an existential norm has roots in Kierkegaard, Heidegger, and Merleau-Ponty, but it has been developed primarily by John Wild. See John Wild, "Authentic Existence," *Ethics*, Vol. LXXV, No. 4 (July, 1965), pp. 227–239, and *The Challenge of Existentialism* (Indiana University Press, 1963), pp. 258 ff.

76. William James, "What Makes a Life Significant?" *Talks to Teachers on Psychology: and to Students on Some of Life's Ideals*, pp. 189–190.

77. William James, *The Meaning of Truth* (Longmans, Green & Co., 1909), p. x.

Selected Bibliography

I. BOOKS BY WILLIAM JAMES (listed in order of publication)

The Principles of Psychology. 2 vols. Henry Holt & Co., Inc., 1890.

Psychology: Briefer Course. Henry Holt & Co., Inc., 1892.

The Will to Believe, and Other Essays in Popular Philosophy. Longmans, Green, & Co., 1897.

Human Immortality: Two Supposed Objections to the Doctrine. Houghton Mifflin Company, 1898.

Talks to Teachers on Psychology: and to Students on Some of Life's Ideals. Henry Holt & Co., Inc., 1899.

The Varieties of Religious Experience: A Study in Human Nature. Longmans, Green, & Co., 1902.

Pragmatism: A New Name for Some Old Ways of Thinking. Longmans, Green, & Co., 1907.

A Pluralistic Universe. Longmans, Green, & Co., 1909.

The Meaning of Truth: A Sequel to "Pragmatism." Longmans, Green, & Co., 1909.

Some Problems of Philosophy: A Beginning of an Introduction to Philosophy, ed. by Henry James, Jr. Longmans, Green, & Co., 1911.

Memories and Studies, ed. by Henry James, Jr. Longmans, Green, & Co., 1911.

Essays in Radical Empiricism, ed. by Ralph Barton Perry. Longmans, Green, & Co., 1912.

Collected Essays and Reviews, ed. by Ralph Barton Perry. Longmans, Green, & Co., 1920.

The Letters of William James, ed. by his son Henry James. 2 vols. Atlantic Monthly Press, 1920.

II. Some Important Books That Deal with William James and His Philosophy

Allen, Gay Wilson, *William James*. The Viking Press, Inc., 1967.

Ayer, A. J., *The Origins of Pragmatism*. Freeman, Cooper and Company, 1968.

Beck, Lewis White, *Six Secular Philosophers*. Harper & Brothers, 1960.

Bixler, Julius Seelye, *Religion in the Philosophy of William James*. Marshall Jones Company, 1926.

Brennan, Bernard P., *The Ethics of William James*. College and University Press Services, Inc., 1962.

Clive, Geoffrey, *The Romantic Enlightenment*. Meridian Books, The World Publishing Company, 1960.

Gurwitsch, Aron, *The Field of Consciousness*. Duquesne University Press, 1964.

Knox, Howard V., *The Philosophy of William James*. Dodge Publishing Company, 1914.

Linschoten, Johannes, *Auf dem Wege zu einer Phänomenologischen Psychologie: Die Psychologie von William James*, tr. from the Dutch by Franz Monk. Berlin: Walter de Gruyter and Company, 1961.

Moore, Edward C., *American Pragmatism: Peirce, James, and Dewey*. Columbia University Press, 1961.

—————— *William James*. Washington Square Press, Inc., 1965.

Passmore, John, *A Hundred Years of Philosophy*. London: Gerald Duckworth & Co., Ltd., 1957.

Perry, Ralph Barton, *Annotated Bibliography of the Writings of William James*. Longmans, Green, & Co., 1920.

—————— *In the Spirit of William James*. Indiana University Press, 1958.

—————— *The Thought and Character of William James*. 2 vols. Little, Brown and Company, 1935.

Reck, Andrew J., *Introduction to William James*. Indiana University Press, 1967.

Roth, Robert J., *American Religious Philosophy*. Harcourt, Brace and World, Inc., 1967.

Royce, Josiah, *William James and Other Essays on the Philosophy of Life*. The Macmillan Company, 1912.

Santayana, George, *Character and Opinion in the United States*. Charles Scribner's Sons, 1924.

Schneider, Herbert W., *A History of American Philosophy*. Columbia University Press, 1946.

Smith, John E., *The Spirit of American Philosophy*. Oxford University Press, Inc., 1963.

Spiegelberg, Herbert, *The Phenomenological Movement*. 2 vols. The Hague: Martinus Nijhoff, 1960.

Stroh, Guy W., *American Philosophy from Edwards to Dewey*. D. Van Nostrand Company, Inc., 1968.

Van Wesep, H. B., *Seven Sages*. Longmans, Green, & Co., 1960.

Wiener, Philip P., *Evolution and the Founders of Pragmatism*. Harper Torchbooks, 1965.

Wild, John, *Existence and the World of Freedom*. Prentice-Hall, Inc., 1963.

——, *The Radical Empiricism of William James*. Doubleday & Company, Inc., 1969.

Wilshire, Bruce, *William James and Phenomenology*. Indiana University Press, 1968.